MARKETING / RESEARCH PEOPLE:
Their Behind-The-Scenes Stories

Jack J. Honomichl

CRAIN
BOOKS

740 RUSH STREET   CHICAGO, IL 60611

Published by Crain Books
A Division of Crain Communications Inc.
740 Rush Street
Chicago, IL 60611

86   85   84   10   9   8   7   6   5   4   3   2   1

ISBN 0-87251-090-5
LC 83-72176

Printed in the United States of America

To Rance Crain, the ideal publisher: He quickly sees the big picture and never quibbles about the details. Without his farsightedness, practically nothing that is in this book would ever have been written.

Contents

Part I

Marketing Case Histories

Foreword

About $66.6 billion is spent for advertising, including direct mail, in the United States each year. Another $7.5 billion, it is estimated, is spent on consumer and trade promotion of packaged goods, and I calculate that about $1.5 billion is spent on marketing, advertising, and public opinion research. Lord knows how much more is spent on other implementers of the marketing process — product publicity, new product development, package design, etc. But, beyond the awesome boxcar budgets, marketing efforts are a drive spring of sorts for our national economy — the font of new and improved products and services that power growth, make jobs, and, ultimately, create prosperity.

This is my personal point of view, and everything in this book finds its roots in my conviction that marketing is one of the most important, engaging, and intrinsically interesting fields of commercial endeavor.

Yet, given its importance, unfortunately little is written on the subject — and lots of what is comes from outsiders looking in. What these people write is often illuminating and worthwhile, but . . . somehow, it seldom does justice to the endeavor as viewed from the inside. That insider's point of view, I hope, is what I have accurately reflected, and appreciated, in the articles that comprise this book.

One reason insiders do not often tell their tales is, of course, confidentiality. Much of the behind-the-scenes work done in marketing is considered proprietary; after all, it's been done at considerable expense with the goal of getting the edge on competition. This is especially true of the marketing and advertising research that is done to develop and perfect marketing plans that, hopefully, are attuned to the wants and needs of some segment of American society. These studies are considered secret, and seldom do the detailed findings find their way into the public press.

3

So, much of what is written in this book would not have been possible without the full cooperation of those top executives who, for the first time, provided a writer access to their private marketing files and studies. Their candor, plus insights from innumerable marketing functionaries who were hands-on participants in the stories being told, have made possible the revelatory writing which, unfortunately, is quite rare. You will find here some marketing philosophy, but mostly it's the workaday, grind-it-out story of marketing professionals, human to the core, doing their job, making almost accidental discoveries that seem brilliant in retrospect, perpetuating mistakes, taking gambles, making end runs around stronger competitors, and — just generally — working in the exciting world of marketing.

This is their story; I am merely the spokesman.

Chapter 1

The Marketing
of Arm & Hammer

The "I've got a secret . . ." advertising campaign that ran for Arm & Hammer baking soda, starting in February 1971, has come to be recognized as a classic. But the full, behind-the-scenes story of how imaginative and aggressive marketing propelled sleepy old Church & Dwight Company, Piscataway, N.J., into extraordinary growth and rejuvenation had never been told before the story appeared in Advertising Age *on September 20, 1982. And, indeed, it would not have been told thoroughly without the full cooperation of Robert A. Davies III, president of Church & Dwight.*

The interview with Mr. Davies, which follows the story, is extraordinarily candid — and revealing. But, due to space limitations in Advertising Age, *their original article left out some of Mr. Davies' comments. The full story follows, and I submit that it is must reading for any aspiring marketing manager.*

I am pleased to note that in the annual Journalism Awards Competition sponsored by Compton Advertising, Inc., which is meant to "honor the writers of those articles [about advertising] which are particularly creative and thought provoking," the Arm & Hammer article won top prize for 1982.

The Marketing Story —
The Product as Hero

The hero of this story is the product, which is a marketing man's dream come true.

The raw material is plentiful and relatively cheap to mine and process. The product itself is a colorless, odorless powder with a slightly salty taste. It has a multitude of uses ranging from an ingredient in cookie recipes to the deodorization of septic tanks, to use on movie sets to simulate snow. Many of its uses have not yet been exploited commercially, and each year thousands of consumers write

5

to tell about new uses they think they've discovered. The product's brand name has unaided recognition among 97 percent of female heads of households in the United States, and the good will it enjoys is awesome. The package is a simple cardboard box, and for all practical purposes, there is no limit on shelf life. Almost all grocery stores stock it. Surveys show that, at any point in time, about 95 percent of all U.S. households have one or more packages in use. There are no branded competitive products of consequence.

Product usage in some, if not all, instances is very responsive to advertising. The marketing strategy since 1980 has been to lower price to give the product an even better cost/value relationship. The biggest problem marketing management has is the broadening of usage through consumer education programs and the development of flanker products — and, more recently, cost competition from no-name generic brands.

This paragon of marketing virtues is Arm & Hammer Baking Soda, a brand marketed by the Arm & Hammer Division of Church & Dwight Company, Inc., Piscataway, N.J. Its affectionate nickname in-house is "mother baking soda," and its history dates back to 1846 when co-founder John Dwight opened a "plant" in his kitchen to process and package the fine white powder that is, technically, sodium bicarbonate, or $NaHCO_3$ in the language of chemistry.

Church & Dwight's net sales in 1982 were expected to be about $150 million, almost a tenfold increase over the level ($15.6 million) in 1969 when the company started its much-publicized product prolif-eration program under the spur of Robert A. Davies III, who came from a group product manager post at Boyle-Midway (division of American Home Products) to become vice president, marketing at Church & Dwight. In 1976 Mr. Davies moved up to vice president/general manager, Arm & Hammer Division, and in March 1981 he was named president and chief operating officer of Church & Dwight.

Up until 1969, Arm & Hammer Baking Soda was a sleepy, one-dimensional brand — albeit a staple on the grocer's shelf — with an advertising budget of less than $500,000 a year, mostly in print. What has happened since then, however, is a fascinating story — the saga of a high-pressure campaign to exploit the venerable Arm & Hammer name and logo by (1) an advertising blitz to promote new uses for the product and accelerate the use-up rate, (2) the development of new flanker items keyed to specific usage/applications, and (3) the crea-tion of entirely new products.

What follows is an insider's story of this campaign, which includes consumer research data and internal C&D figures never before made public. And if you're one of those many people who has always been a mite hazy about what this thing called "marketing" is all about, hang on; you're about to get a cram course that should make it perfectly clear.

Cool Sales Spur

The single most dramatic move Arm & Hammer made — and the one, of course, that has received most attention in the press — was the stimulation, via advertising, of an extended use for baking soda, namely putting an open box inside a refrigerator as an air freshener/ deodorant.

Advertising was prepared by Arm & Hammer's agency (Kelly, Nason at the time; it's now defunct), and a test was run in 1972 on a network TV West Coast feed. (In the balance of the country, the company was then airing a commercial boosting baking soda for light-duty cleaning chores.) Table 1-1 shows the dramatic results of that test, as measured by tracking surveys done via telephone. Eventually, the penetration numbers leveled off at about 80 percent.

Well, you gotta believe the early results of that test got the marketing adrenalin flowing back at the home office. "Our brokers started calling in," recalls Burton B. Staniar, who had come from Colgate-Palmolive to C&D in 1970 as a group business manager, "and they said the shelves were empty; there were out-of-stock problems all over the West Coast. We knew we had discovered gold."

Quite naturally, Arm & Hammer moved quickly to get that refrigerator copy onto the total network, and results (shown in Table 1-2) were equally dramatic. Eventually, these numbers leveled off at about 90 percent.

The bottom line is that in 1971 C&D sold 2,300,000 equivalent 24-pound cases of Arm & Hammer Baking Soda into grocery channels. In 1974, it sold 3,965,000 cases. That's a 72 percent increase, and almost all of it was due to the refrigerator deodorant campaign.

A logical extension of this very successful move was to go a step further — run advertising to suggest that another box of Arm &

Table 1-1

% Households Saying They Have Used Baking Soda in Refrigerator as a Deodorant (West Coast)	
May 1973	63
March 1973	57
October 1972	43
June 1972	38
May 1972	27
February 1972	19

Table 1-2

% Households Saying They Have Used Baking Soda in Refrigerator as an Air Freshener/Deodorant (Total U.S.)	
March 1973	57
October 1972	45
June 1972	38
February 1972	1

Hammer Baking Soda be put inside the refrigerator's freezer compartment for the same purpose. Table 1-3 shows how that expanded usage campaign produced.

Successful as these campaigns were, they also pointed up a weakness in the refrigerator/deodorizer usage pattern, namely: A woman might go for the concept, buy a box of baking soda, put it into the refrigerator (or freezer), and then forget it. It could sit there for months, and that didn't induce repeat purchasing. So, how to speed up that process? The answer was advertising designed to get the box out of the refrigerator. The idea was that after the box of Arm & Hammer had worked in the refrigerator for a while, remove it and pour the contents down the kitchen drain to deodorize it too. Table 1-4 shows the results of that limited campaign.

Behind the Campaign

"There are at least ten guys running around New York claiming some credit for the refrigerator campaign idea," says Gerald Schoenfeld, president of Gerald Schoenfeld, Inc., a consulting firm specializing in new product concepts. He should know; Mr. Schoenfeld is the most conspicuous of the ten. You may have noted the advertisements his firm runs in *Advertising Age*; the headline is "Who Put Baking Soda in the Refrigerator?"

Back in 1969-1976, however, Mr. Schoenfeld was president of Kelly, Nason, and creator of the now-famous refrigerator commercial, "I've got a secret . . . [in the refrigerator]." In addition to Mr.

Table 1-3

% Households Saying They Have Used Baking Soda in Refrigerator Freezer as a Deodorant (Total U.S.)	
1981	28
1980	24
1979	18
1978	12

Schoenfeld, I've also talked with Reynald M. Swift, who in 1971 came from American Cyanamid to C&D as product manager on baking soda. Between the two, I have tried to piece together the true story of how that West Coast test came to be, and, hopefully, it will serve to dispel the many "personalized" versions that now circulate.

Circa 1969/1970, many focus groups were exploring new product use concepts, and most of the attention was on the cleaning applications of baking soda. Among other things, recalls Mr. Schoenfeld, who moderated many of the groups himself, respondents were exposed to some of the very earliest print ads for Arm & Hammer, one of which promoted the use of baking soda for cleaning the inside walls of iceboxes.

"The idea was in existence when I came aboard," adds Mr. Swift; "it already had project status. But it was nothing new; 'put some in the refrigerator' was a usage suggestion on Arm & Hammer boxes back in the mid-1930s." He also notes that, historically, baking soda had been widely accepted as a mild cleanser for the cleaning of refrigerator surfaces, so it was a short and logical bridge for the consumer to accept use of it to clean the air too.

"The theme of sweetening, freshening kept coming up [in focus groups]," recalls Mr. Schoenfeld, "but at first I didn't pay much attention; we were concentrating on cleaning ideas. It kept coming up, though, and I started to get excited that we might be on to something."

"When we put the proposition to respondents directly — 'Your refrigerator smells, and baking soda will cure that' — it didn't go over at all," says Mr. Swift. "But when we came through the back door and worded the proposition in such a way that it didn't imply the woman was a lousy housekeeper, they showed a lot of interest in the idea." That realization led to Mr. Schoenfeld's oblique "I've got a secret..." copy.

One hunch expressed by Mr. Schoenfeld is that some women feel guilty that they do not clean their refrigerator as often as they think

Table 1-4

% Households Saying They Have Used Baking Soda in the Drain of Their Sink as a Deodorizer (Total U.S.)	
June 1977	67
January 1977	62
July 1976	53
April 1976	46
November 1975	43

they should. Putting a box of baking soda inside at least cleans the air, and that alleviates some of the guilt — and no work is required.

Not everyone at C&D was enthusiastic about the idea — especially the old guard — and, as Mr. Staniar recalls, "It was just one of dozens of ideas we were considering. The important thing is the strategic decision, featuring just one use in advertising instead of several and going onto network television."

In any case, momentum for testing the refrigerator copy on-air kept building amongst the C&D marketing group, and the result was a cause célèbre in American marketing history. As for Mr. Schoenfeld, he told me, "It's been a meal ticket for me."

Previous Expansion Efforts

Famous as the refrigerator caper is, it was not the first attempt by Mr. Davies and the company to expand the usage of Arm & Hammer Baking Soda. A network TV campaign in 1971 promoted its use in bath water to smooth dry, flaky skin, and, as noted, a commercial promoting household cleaning chores was on-air nationwide in 1972. Together, these experiments in single-use advertising and television had produced a sales increase of about 10 percent.

But both of these efforts were overshadowed by an even more ambitious — and audacious — move to broaden the Church & Dwight business base. In 1970, Mr. Davies decided to exploit a growing public concern with ecology by introducing a non-polluting laundry detergent under the Arm & Hammer name, a move not so surprising when you know that, prior to Boyle-Midway, Mr. Davies had been a product manager in the Household Products Division of Colgate-Palmolive. (Before that, he was a salesman with Procter & Gamble.) But when a company with annual revenues of about $16 million takes on P&G and Colgate in their most important product category . . . that's gutsy (or, if you should fail, stupid).

You may recall that at the time there was considerable public concern about phosphates in detergents feeding algae growth in public streams, and products that were not biodegradable were being banned in grocery stores in some communities.

Arm & Hammer Heavy Duty Detergent — which, incidentally, has never had a baking soda ingredient — found immediate acceptance. "We had a $25 million business almost overnight," says Mr. Staniar. In some markets, share of market topped 10 percent, and nationally the brand today still holds about a 3 percent share although it is not in full distribution. (In 1981, this product was restaged; price was lowered, and a "value price too" strategy was adopted.)

Church & Dwight's sales had gone from $15.6 million in 1969 to $57.9 million five years later. Given that this had been achieved by a brash bunch of new marketing employees — recruited from General Foods, Block Drug, P&G, Colgate-Palmolive, and American Cyanamid — who had faced up to P&G and held their own and who had launched one of the most successful advertising campaigns in history, it is not surprising that a giddy attitude of "we can do anything with the Arm & Hammer name" had come to prevail at Church & Dwight. Obviously, it had become difficult for the "old guard" to oppose new ideas, no matter how off-the-wall they might have seemed, and growth was largely self-financing.

In this atmosphere then came an avalanche of new business-building moves, which can be grouped as follows:

- *Promoting increases in established uses for the basic baking soda, mostly via suggested uses on package and advertising.*
  Cleaning kitchen surfaces; additive to bath water; baking ingredient; laundry additive; and general household cleaning chores.

- *Creating new uses for basic baking soda, again mostly by advertising and suggestions on package.*
  Refrigerator/freezer air deodorant; cat litter deodorant; dog deodorant; water treatment in swimming pools; septic tank deodorant; kitchen drain deodorant; and as a dentifrice (plaque removal claim).

- *Development of flanker products—basic baking soda in special packaging aimed at specific use segments.*
  Rug/carpet deodorizer; cat litter deodorizer; and a kitchen cleaner that failed.

- *Development of entirely new products, capitalizing on the Arm & Hammer name / logo.*
  Heavy-duty laundry detergent; oven cleaner; liquid detergent; and two conspicuous failures — a spray underarm deodorant and a spray disinfectant.

Some packaging innovations also stemmed from this effort — for instance, the introduction of a 4-pound box of Arm & Hammer Baking Soda to tie in with heavy use applications, such as swimming pools and septic tanks, and the creation of entirely new packaging, which, in the case of cat litter deodorizer, got baking soda into the supermarket's pet food section, near cat box litter.

Research Guidance

Sifting and evaluating so many new ideas — plus many more that died aborning — suggests a considerable amount of consumer and marketing research, and Church & Dwight has had a very active program, spending about $500,000 a year, on average. But to this day, C&D does not have a marketing research staffer.

In lieu of the traditional research setup, C&D has since 1971 funnelled almost all its research — well over 150 studies at this point — through one research firm, Behavioral Analysis, Inc., in Irvington, N.Y., and its president, Richard Reiser.

"We've done just about every kind of study there is," says Mr. Reiser, citing segmentation studies, tracking of usage and awareness, on-air and off-air copy testing, product placement tests, price elasticity studies, promotion testing, image studies, and — obviously — concept testing, some of which has been focused on special ownership segments like septic tank or swimming pool owners.

"This continuity is important," notes Mr. Reiser, "because we've been able to build up a comprehensive body of knowledge that probably wouldn't result from a bunch of unrelated, ad hoc studies. Also, we've wasted little time and money in studying the same phenomenon twice."

The Bottom Line

Behavioral Analysis, Inc., on the basis of studies they've conducted, estimates how much of the basic Arm & Hammer Baking Soda volume is consumed by end-use applications in the home. (These estimates *do not* include plus-volume gained via flankers or new products; they just relate to the basic Yellow Box volume, which in turn accounted for about one-third of total Church & Dwight dollar volume in 1981.)

Back in 1970, the year of departure, Yellow Box volume was 2.3 million cases. BAI estimates for that year say that the single most important end use was cleaning refrigerator surfaces, which accounted for about one-third of the tonnage. The second most important uses were bath water treatment and general household cleaning. Other important end uses were as a skin rash treatment, deodorizer, and the cleaning of teeth. Use in baking, it is estimated, accounted for only 6 percent of end-use volume, which might be surprising since the product is called "baking soda."

By 1981, case volume on Yellow Box had grown to 5 million cases. But now the main end use, by far, was to deodorize refrigerator air, which accounted for about 25 percent. The second most important use was general household cleaning, and secondary uses were bath water treatment, cleaning refrigerator surfaces, skin rash treatment, rug deodorizer, cat box litter deodorizer, kitchen drain deodorizer, septic tank deodorizer, swimming pool treatment, etc.

In 1981, baking still accounted for 6 percent of the estimated end-use consumption, but, since the base had doubled, it meant that over twice as many cases were being used for that purpose. And that's an interesting result of all the promotion — the introduction of new uses did not take from the established uses of 1970; if anything, it expanded the tonnage they represented, if not the relative importance.

"If we had done anything less," says Mr. Staniar, "it would have been a failure. The Arm & Hammer name has such phenomenal strength, such good equity, it was hard to do anything wrong. Even if we screwed up — as we did with the underarm deodorant, that was a bad product — the consumer forgave us."

"The Arm & Hammer name, in fact, presents a very serious research problem," says Mr. Reiser. "Whenever we associate it with a new product or concept, consumer acceptance and 'will buy' intentions are always unrealistically high; consumers are reluctant to reject Arm & Hammer. Factoring down to the reality of the situation is always difficult."

(In 1975, Helene Curtis Industries, Inc. edged too close to the magic Arm & Hammer name by marketing an underarm deodorant called "Arm and Arm Deodorant." Church & Dwight brought a trademark infringement suit and won. The settlement of $2 million in 1979 was one of the largest in U.S. legal history.)

The Current Situation

A concern at Arm & Hammer currently is the importance of no-name, generic baking sodas; these products now have about 10 percent of the category volume. This has led Church & Dwight to emphasize the word "pure" on boxes (reminiscent of the Bayer aspirin effort some years back to further differentiate their product from low-price competition by stressing quality control), the lowering of price (twice within the past two years), and an ever-growing use of trade and consumer deals, including coupons.

This situation, of course, spurs even further efforts to develop "enhanced" baking soda-based products that cannot so easily be duplicated by manufacturers of the basic soda ash.

On the brighter side, Mr. Davies is presently very enthusiastic about a new use for baking soda: When it is added to cow feed, the cows reportedly produce more and better milk. Now, when you stop to think about how many milk cows are being fed every day...maybe, just maybe, the refrigerator deodorant campaign might turn out to be the second most important case history at Church & Dwight.

The Arm & Hammer Baking Soda box, once simplistic, is now a montage of marketing elements, partly because of an increasingly competitive environment. One pound box like this can contain (1) proof-of-purchase seal; (2) a cookie recipe; (3) money-back guarantee statement; (4) usage (deodorizer and cleanser) suggestions and instructions; (5) a cook book ("All Time Baking Soda Favorites") offer; and (6) usage directions as an antacid. The familiar Arm-and-Hammer logo is one link to the past; it has been in use on baking soda since 1867.

Baking Soda:
What Is It? How Does It Work?

Baking soda is a derivative of trona ore. One of the richest deposits in the United States is located from 600 to 2,400 feet below ground in southwestern Wyoming, where Church & Dwight has its largest production facility. These deposits were an accidental find, the by-product of gas and oil exploration drilling in the 1930s.

Technically, trona ore is a mineral composed of about 85 percent sodium sesquicarbonate — a hard crystal-like material. It is mined much like coal and brought to the surface through deep shafts. The ore is crushed and heated to about 500° F. to burn off foreign materials and convert it to sodium carbonate, or soda ash as it is most commonly known. The yield is about 60 percent. Church & Dwight purchases soda ash and then in its own plants reacts it with water and carbon dioxide to produce sodium bicarbonate, or baking soda — a granular substance that is colorless and odorless with a characteristic salty taste.

The job baking soda does in eliminating odors inside a refrigerator, for instance, is best understood if you think of odors as chemicals, whose presence in the air can be measured. ("But the instruments we use aren't as sensitive as a human nose," says Dr. Richard Lehne, director of corporate regulatory affairs at Church & Dwight. "The average nose is still the best instrument made to detect odors.")

Some such odors are acidic and have a negative electrical charge while some are basic with a positive electrical charge; both are neutralized by baking soda. Other odors, the nonionic or neutral ones, are absorbed in a sponge-like process. At any time, a refrigerator could have all three types of odors or chemicals in the air, and the deodorization process going on is quite complex.

"In fact," says Dr. Lehne, "we're not completely familiar with the entire mechanism, despite considerable testing. In any case, the process is so effective that even if a box of baking soda weren't opened, odors would be filtered right through the cardboard and absorbed/neutralized. Also baking soda has a finite chemical life, but it does not start to work its absorbent magic and lose this life until an odor is in the air to react with it."

In a "normal" refrigerator, with "normal" odors, tests show a one-pound box of baking soda can absorb/neutralize about two months worth of odor chemicals.

Human bodies also manufacture sodium bicarbonate, which helps to maintain the proper acid-base balance in the blood stream. When you take an antacid with sodium bicarbonate, what you are doing, in effect, is supplying a concentrated dose of sodium bicarbonate directly into the excess stomach acid that the body has been unable to neutralize in a "normal" fashion. Incidentally, notice and description of sodium bicarbonate as a pharmaceutical product first appeared in U.S. medical literature in 1840.

In baking, baking soda serves as a leavening agent since, when heated or put in contact with an acidic material, it produces gaseous carbon dioxide and a sodium salt. Baking soda also works as a cleaner, since it is a mild alkali which, when mixed with fatty acids normally found in dirt and grease, makes a form of soap. This "soap" in turn cleans, aided by a gentle abrasive texture.

And what happens when milady adds baking soda to her bath water? The human skin is always growing, and the top layer consists of hard protein scales (called keratin), which feel flaky. Baking soda reacts with the keratin in a softening process, and the result is a smooth-feeling skin. How does it work? "We're not exactly sure," says Dr. Lehne, "but it does a good job."

According to Dr. Lehne, no single man-made substance could do all the jobs baking soda does as effectively; it would take several such products.

Bob Davies Looks Back:
"If I had it to do over again"

Robert A. Davies III came to Church & Dwight in 1969 as vice president/marketing in the Arm & Hammer Division. In 1976, he became general manager of the Arm & Hammer Division, and in 1981, president of Church & Dwight Company.

In August, 1982, I interviewed Mr. Davies at Church & Dwight headquarters in Piscataway, N.J., during which he reflected on the past 13 years, the good and bad decisions, and the advice he'd give to other companies interested in a broad new-product expansion program.

Honomichl: Looking back, if you had it to do over again, what would you do differently?
Davies: First of all, I'm kind of pleased with what we've done. But if I had to do it over again? Well, I think of a series of things. The first thing I would have done is recognize the value of baking soda itself as a brand much earlier because we spent fully the first two or three years working on anything but baking soda. There was a fair amount

of wasted money in there, certainly a lot of wasted time, a lack of focus.

There was a going-in assumption that the strength here was the brand name, Arm & Hammer, and there was an equal assumption that baking soda was an unexciting product in and of itself that was profitable and could generate some money, but had little value in terms of building the brand. I think the number one thing is to have recognized that earlier.

A second thing is that I would have moved slower. We were in a great rush to be successful and to proceed, and to grow, and to develop. When I joined the company, it was only very modestly profitable in relation to its operations; the profitability it enjoyed was mainly the result of its portfolio, its investments. There was a great rush to get the operating business larger and more profitable, and this caused mistakes to be made, caused some products to be marketed that should not have been marketed, caused a lot of marketing development dollars — both in R&D technology and marketing research — to be spent that need not have been spent. It caused products to go to market before they were ready to go to market, and it caused some decisions to expand broadly when the proper thing to do was to continue test marketing. So, the second thing would be to not have rushed nearly as much.

A third thing I would have done, which is consistent with the second, is that I wouldn't have staffed nearly as rapidly. I built a lot of staff quite early, and the staff began to take on a life of its own to justify its existence. We were able to attract extraordinarily bright and talented people to the company — quite frankly, more people than we could possibly keep busy and consume and find resourceful jobs for — and too many people working on a problem is, I guess, every bit as bad, if not worse than — in fact, I'll say it was worse — than too few people working on a problem.

At one point in time — gee, I don't remember for sure — not too long after I was here, maybe after three years, we must have had 10 or 12 people in the marketing department. That was a lot of people given the status of the business. We were always staffing to meet next year's, or the following year's, or three years' from now perceived needs. And that didn't further the perceived development of the business; in fact, I think it tended to hinder us, to tie us up.

A fourth thing I would have done — I went through a period when I relinquished too much authority to the marketing organization. I had this relatively large group of talented, energetic, hardworking, resourceful, inventive people, and I was a young guy — I was in my mid-30s at that point in time — and I went through a period where I thought it was a good, sound management practice to get best results by giving lots and lots of authority to very capable people. That's a very positive practice to energize people, to turn them on, making them alive and resourceful and what not, but if you don't at the same time use your own experience base and judgment and keep very careful control on what is going on, a lot of dollars and time can be wasted. There was a period — three or four years — when I went too far down that road; I think that was an error.

I would be very, very careful in the new products area (I don't think this comment is equally applicable to established products) — to acting on a situation in the interests of competitive pressure — I'd be very, very careful of that. At one time, we saw some of our good ideas being snapped up by competitors or would-be competitors, and, of course, when you see your idea about to be implemented by somebody else, this gets the hackles up; not only are you afraid you're going to lose the opportunity, but there is a whole emotional thing that overrides, that says, "By heavens, we've been working on this idea, and no one else should do anything with baking soda except this company." This precipitated some decision-making that turned out not to be sound for the company. I would be very, very cautious making decisions in the new product area because of competitive pressure. With established products, I think that would be a poor rule; if you don't react to competition in your established products, you'll be dead.

Honomichl: What do you regard, in retrospect, to be the largest single mistake you made?

Davies: The most costly error we made was to go national with personal deodorant at a time that wasn't appropriate, with a product that wasn't ready to go to market, with a selling proposition that wasn't finely honed, with what I think turned out to be the wrong form of product; that was the most costly error we made, in terms of costs you can see.

However, the larger error — one that I've already touched on — was maybe in simply not moving more slowly, more deliberately, in terms of organization, structure, strategy, product development — following the principle that a more deliberate, measured, careful approach will get you ahead further. It's the tortoise and hare story.

Honomichl: Wouldn't that have lost you some of your momentum, the enthusiasm that was building up?

Davies: I'm sure we would have lost something, but if you stop and think that if with that you had staffed for a more deliberate and slow approach — and I don't mean to communicate that the place would have become a sleepy little corner; that's not part of my thinking — but a more measured, deliberate, studied approach — crawling before walking, walking before running — I think it could have been on a basis that would still have been exciting. Could be wrong.

Honomichl: Weren't the people around here, including yourself, terrified at the prospect of a $15 million company facing up to Procter and Colgate in their home turf, in their biggest and most important product category?

Davies: To answer that perfectly honestly, I think we weren't all smart enough; we should have been more concerned about that than we were. At the time, we were not.

Honomichl: A lot of people out there probably have thought about doing something similar but backed off because they were afraid of the consequences. What would you advise them? You're one of the few people who have gotten away with it.

Davies: Give it a shot — if — if you have some kind of basic strength that can carry the day through. If you're up against Procter, you're probably not going to enjoy any cost advantage, or any marketing or advertising or sales clout. You have to have an edge. We had an edge: the Arm & Hammer name.

Honomichl: And you could move more quickly; they can be muscle bound in many respects.

Davies: That's true; they were particularly tied up in their policies regarding phosphate at that time.

Honomichl: And it's particularly interesting in that you were working through brokers.

Davies: Oh, yeah. I think very highly of brokers. Procter & Gamble enjoys a lesser cost sales organization; their cost of sales compared to ours — as a percentage of sales dollars — would be approximately half of ours. That's a nice advantage. However, in terms of effectiveness, I think very highly of food brokers. Church & Dwight has been able to attract a very, very fine group of brokers; seldom has our sales force let us down.

Honomichl: You have the traditional regional salesmen setup?

Davies: We have about eight regional salesmen of our own and a national sales manager. And we have a national field sales manager to handle non-food, and then about 80 food brokers.

Honomichl: Do you think the Arm & Hammer act would travel? Could you take it into international markets? Or is it so native American that it wouldn't travel?

Davies: Well, are you talking about baking soda under the Arm & Hammer name?

Honomichl: Yes, and for pretty much the same uses.

Davies: We've spent a fair amount of time assessing that, and certainly there is no clear-cut answer; it's never been tried. And it's no lead-pipe cinch, or we would have tried. I think there's a decent chance; it's a 50-50 kind of chance. There are some definite problems. Baking soda is indigenous to this country; it's part of the root structure of Americana. But it is sold in some other countries in some channels of distribution, food and drug stores in Germany and France. But its volume base is miniscule as compared to this country.

Honomichl: I've gotten the impression that this cow feed additive thing could be bigger than everything else some day. You could be on the verge of another historic leap ahead in volume.

Davies: That is possible. But that's a technical question; that's sheerly based on the technology, the functionality of the product.

Honomichl: As based on productivity — increased production related to cost?

Davies: Yes. We are doing a lot of work in this area, and we enjoy a nice dairy business. But to take on the dimensions of what you indicated, we would be required to go a good deal further — which is possible.

Honomichl: What's coming next? What are you working on now — that you can talk about?

Davies: Well, we're testing a liquid laundry detergent under the value strategy in New York state right now, and that brand is doing fairly well. That's under evaluation as to where that will lead us. Could be that over time there will be other things of that nature.

The name itself — Arm & Hammer — we regard to be an underutilized asset. In terms of baking soda, we still see the future as infinite — baking soda or baking soda new products. Baking soda is used for about 15 different basic use areas, and then it breaks down to literally hundreds of uses from those areas. And we've only tapped into a few of the basic ones so far. I regard that as a mine where we've only tapped the first vein. There are a lot more veins; I don't know how many more, but a lot more.

Honomichl: Have the big guys in the grocery business tried to buy you? I assume you would have been a hot acquisition prospect — a tightly held company with a great growth record.

Davies: Dwight handles that [Dwight C. Minton, chairman of the board and chief executive officer], but I think it's safe to say there is a level of interest that is fairly constant. But we're very much oriented to running our own business, and I think we're doing a reasonably creditable job of doing it so we don't encourage that sort of thing at all.

Honomichl: You have a company that is, as I understand it, controlled about 70 percent in-house. What difference has that made? Could you, Bob Davies, have done what you did here in a larger, more broadly held company?

Davies: I think it might have been difficult. I think you're onto a key point. I think the strength of the company is its shareholder group; it's very, very loyal.

A lot of the shareholders are third, fourth — I suppose even fifth — generation Churches and Dwights who regard their stock with a certain family pride, so they take a slightly different, more long-term attitude towards the property. This has been a definite, clear strength to the company.

Honomichl: What was the role of marketing research in all this? Was it a driving force or a supportive force?

Davies: It was a guiding force; it wasn't a leadership force.

Honomichl: You have done something rare; you've never built up an internal market research staff, and you've placed all your research work with one firm.

Davies: It enabled us to, on a constant basis, relate to an extraordinarily capable individual, Dick Reiser, who has been very, very helpful to us. However, I'll say that the help has been in counseling, guidance advice, observation as opposed to a prime moving force. On the whole, it's been good, sound advice and research as opposed to a leadership position in terms of what we should do — but it has had some elements of leadership.

Honomichl: Would you recommend that approach to other companies the same size of Church & Dwight?

Davies: I would be very cautious in a company of our size of an internal marketing research capability. This company could not attract or hold on to the talent of a fellow like Dick Reiser; even if the expense would be warranted, which it probably would be, the individual wouldn't be interested. He would become disenchanted; it wouldn't be enough for him. He would become bored. So, I definitely would advise it — assuming one has a fellow the quality of Dick Reiser available to him.

Honomichl: Has Church & Dwight — with its growth — become an R&D oriented company?

Davies: We regard the company in many respects to be a technology company and make a major commitment. That commitment has grown a fair amount in the past year or two; it's been much higher in recent years. We had no technological capabilities 13, 14 years ago.

The issue is the degree to which you inherently believe you have potential in your business. We believe there is a fair amount in sodium bicarbonate and we can pursue it — and we realize that here we are working an area that has not been very heavily worked in American industry.

Honomichl: What would you tell all those other marketing guys who watch Church & Dwight and say, "That's what we should be doing"?

Davies: My first thought goes to all those people who have done better than we have done. There are some very successful operations that have taken place in the last 10 years.

Remember, we started with a small base. When I came here in 1969, sales were about $16 million. Earnings were modest. But the company had a dynamite product, baking soda, and a dynamite name, Arm & Hammer. So, we started with sound assets.

The real question is "What did we do right?" First of all, we tried. I've been critical about some of the things we did wrong, but you can only do that if you've been trying. You've got to have the basic enthusiasm. You've got to have the drive, you've got to have the will, you have to get out there and be willing to make errors. We had a lot of that; we had it in spades.

Honomichl: Do you think that could be accomplished in a very large company?

Davies: Yes, I expect it could. You can get a business unit charged up — I think it has to do with excitement and leadership and vision. I think one of the things I've done well here is to constantly stir up things, constantly have people excited. We've had some bad times, tough times, but it's fun to come to work — and we've had an atmosphere where new thinking, including unconventional thinking, is welcome. You can do that in a large organization, but it's easier in a small organization.

Another thing we've done right would be not to assume that there is not opportunity right in what you're doing right now. Too often, I think, you take a look at your business and you orient yourself to the problems; you can spend all your time focusing on the problems. You never go to a joy meeting, okay? You can get pretty down on things. To allow yourself as a result to fail to see the inherent opportunities in what you already have, and what you already are, and what you already possess, is a mistake. The fine group of people we had working on baking soda before we got going on it thought they reasonably had done everything that could be done. In fact, I myself spent the first two or three years assuming that was the case. So, don't overlook the possibility that there is opportunity in what you're doing right now.

Chapter 2

How Detroit Reacted
to the Imported Car Threat

In the spring of 1980, when it was cruelly evident that the U.S. automobile industry had been devastated and that one of the main reasons was its slack, apparently ill-informed response to the growing flood of well-made and relatively cheap imported cars, Rance Crain, editor of Advertising Age, *asked me to do a piece on the subject. I was to try to determine just where, when, and why Detroit's marketing efforts lost touch with the American consumer, or — as Mr. Crain summarized it — "How did they ever get into such a mess?"*

I spent four months on the article, which finally appeared in Advertising Age *on August 4, 1980. The story traced back to 1953, when American Motors introduced the Rambler, a car positioned as a gas saver. Detroit laughed.*

Most of my information came from executives — marketing and marketing research — who held key, bird's-eye positions in the U.S. auto industry from 1950 to 1970. The idea was to learn what they knew about how the U.S. auto market was changing at the time, and how top management reacted. It's a grim story, especially when you realize that once upon a time, the auto industry was estimated to account for about 18 percent of our country's Gross National Product.

In retrospect, I pulled my punches in this article; it should have been more critical of Detroit's apparent lack of regard for product quality and quality control; in that respect, they held the door open for the Germans and Japanese.

Early Background — The Compacts

Here's the U.S. auto industry bent double. Over 28 percent of the Big Three's workers are idle, dividends are being cut, and by year's end [end of 1980], it is estimated, 11 major plants will have been closed and one-fourth of the industry's dealer franchises will have filed for bankruptcy. Our third largest auto maker is now being managed by the federal government; the second largest is in deep financial trouble.

How in the world did an industry that accounts for about 18 percent of our country's GNP get into such a bind — a bind that probably will get worse before it gets better?

In dire circumstances like these, there's a natural tendency to pile the main blame onto the top management of Detroit's Big Three — Ford, General Motors, and Chrysler. They were out of touch with the consumer; slow to react to the growing demand for small, fuel-efficient cars; and prone to underestimate the marketing prowess of foreign exporters like Nissan, Toyota, Volkswagen, Peugeot, et al.

In retrospect, there's some truth in all that. The full story, however, is far, far more complex and traces all the way back to the early 1950s when American Motors introduced the Rambler to compete with the "gas-guzzling dinosaurs" favored by Detroit's Big Three.

In an attempt to put today's predicament into perspective, to get the full story on how the small, economy-car phenomenon evolved in the U.S. auto market, and to identify turning-point decisions along the way, I have recently interviewed numerous auto executives, most of whom held key executive positions in Big Three companies or their advertising agencies back in the 1950s, 1960s, and 1970s, and some, currently. Many of these informants worked in marketing research and, hence, were privy to marketing information that was available — and how top management reacted to it.

Out of this, a fascinating story has unfolded, and if there are lessons to be learned, it seems to me they are:

1. Today's situation didn't just happen; it evolved over time.

2. The U.S. auto industry is living with some very cruel economic facts of life.

3. Some courses of action, easily espoused by outsiders — including the federal government — are in fact very difficult, expensive, and time-consuming for the auto industry to implement.

4. The same thing could happen to your business; learn from it.

The Dinosaur

A gallon of regular gasoline was selling for 26.8 cents a gallon, on average, in 1953 when George Romney, the feisty, outspoken, and — in retrospect — prophetic president of American Motors introduced his Rambler. The selling proposition: many Americans wanted a relatively spartan, gas-conservative car. To Detroit's surprise, Rambler sales took off — despite a relatively weak dealer network. One GM agency executive on the scene at the time recently told me, "GM's top management couldn't believe it; they thought it was a fluke."

To put things into perspective, in 1952, 30,000 foreign-made cars — mostly British — were being imported into the United States, and they accounted for less than 1 percent of new car registrations. This dropped to 28,000 in '53, and to 23,000 in '54, the year, incidentally, when VW's famous Beetle first moved to the top of the import list with 5,000 units.

It was in 1955 that the Paley Commission, now nearly forgotten, made its report on strategic minerals to Congress. A major finding was that, in due course, the United States faced a shortage of oil. Some Big Three executives believed this too.

Eventually, the Rambler was withdrawn from the market, but a point had been made, and this was not lost on the Big Three. "It was in the mid-50s," recalls George H. Brown, who was marketing research manager for the Ford division of Ford Motor Company at the time, "that the concept of market segmentation started to be recognized in Detroit."

Charlie Brown's Falcon

By 1958, when a gallon of regular gasoline sold for nearly 30 cents, the annual imports of foreign-made cars had increased by 16 times their 1953 level to 380,000 units — and Detroit was ready to launch its first major counterattack: Ford's little economy car, the Falcon, and its kissin' cousin, the Mercury Comet.

The decision to tool and go into full-scale production of a "compact" was made in 1957, and the Falcon was introduced to Ford dealers on September 2, 1959, via a closed-circuit telecast in 21 cities, and to the general public via a 20-page section in the *New York Times* on October 4.

J. Walter Thompson Company was the agency, and they made Charlie Brown, the "Peanuts" cartoon character, the spokesman for Falcon. The marketing plan called for a whimsical Charlie Brown newsletter, which was mailed to hundreds of thousands of foreign car owners. The production goal for Falcon was 97,000 units by year's end.

George Brown, who headed Ford's research on the Falcon, in a speech before the Detroit chapter of the American Marketing Association in December, 1959, reported on 14 research studies that led to the Falcon production decision. He said:

> In the early part of 1958 it was quite apparent sales of domestic cars were dropping while sales of foreign cars had picked up and were rising.

This was about the time we were reading charges in newspapers and magazine articles that the auto manufacturers were failing to anticipate consumer preferences. This is not true. Research had already been long under way — but was under wraps. Ford began to act at a very early date, first analyzing the foreign car competition as far back as 1953.

We knew . . . that foreign cars were selling in considerable volume in some market areas, or pockets, and had attained 1.5 percent of the total market. This was projected to envision a future 6 percent.

What do people want? Broadly, it figured out like this. They wanted such a car to be just like the standard car, but it should cost only $1,500 and travel 30 miles on a gallon of gas.

As we went along, we became convinced the market for the economy car was a cross-section of the total car market.

Remember, this was 15 years before the first oil embargo, and most Americans had never heard of Saudi Arabia, let alone Iran.

Mr. Brown recently told me the Falcon was a tough sell to Ford's top management, who cited the bad sales experience with their own small cars that had been imported into the U.S.

It's important to recognize that during the 1950s, Detroit's Big Three were well established in the European small car market. GM subsidiaries in Germany were making the Cadet and the Opel and, in England, the Vauxhall. Ford had the English Ford. Chrysler, in 1956, bought an interest in Simca, Inc., the French auto manufacturer. Hence, Detroit was well aware of the production economics — and profit possibilities — of small, high-milage cars, designed as they were for countries where gasoline cost much more than in the United States.

And that gets us to **Economic Fact of Life No. 1:** It was natural, at first, for Detroit to try to import its own small cars into the United States; the production nut was already covered by sales in Europe and other parts of the world, and an import represented variable costs only. There would be no need to expend the millions of dollars necessary to tool up for manufacture of similar cars inside the United States.

These same economies, of course, work for the German and Japanese auto manufacturers too, and that made it relatively easy (read "inexpensive") for them to penetrate the United States market later on.

But early efforts to import and sell such cars as the Opel and Vauxhall through GM's Buick and Pontiac dealers fell flat; only about 25 percent would handle the little imports. And that brings us to

Economic Fact of Life No. 2: Standard American cars offered dealers a "profit potential," as they say in Detroit, of from 23 to 25 percent; small economy cars offered only 15 to 17 percent. So, for each small car sold at the expense of a larger one, the dealer lost revenue, both in absolute and relative terms.

And that gets us to *Economic Fact of Life No. 3:* The auto manufacturers' true customer is the dealer; if he's not excited about a new car offering, he can resist, drag his sales feet. And auto dealers tend to be short-term thinkers, intent on weekly — make that daily — sales and cash flow. The top management of Detroit's Big Three through the 1950s and '60s were extraordinarily sensitive to the opinions of the people who owned their dealerships, and relatively blasé about the ultimate consumer's wants and needs.

U.S. News Story

An item of note took place in 1958, just about a year before the Falcon introduction. *U.S. News & World Report* magazine published a study, done by Benson & Benson, Inc., in Princeton, regarding the auto preferences of Americans. This quote from *Advertising Age* tells the story:

> The Detroit auto wizards who have been hopefully assuming the small foreign car market in the U.S. is an off-beat market of atypical buyers, hence no serious threat to domestic car makers, will derive no joy from a small car report just published. . .
>
> The market for small foreign cars is virtually the same market for new domestic cars — mostly the upper income managerial and professional families — the report concludes.

This study went on to say that, among those who planned to buy a new car within the near future, the favored brand among both foreign and domestic makes was Volkswagen, which was named first by 28 percent of the respondents. Following, in order, were Chevy, Ford, and Mr. Romney's Rambler.

The general reaction in Detroit, I have been told, was: "That's what consumers say, but once they get into the showroom, they trade up." And, indeed, there was a great deal of truth in that.

It is important to pause here and recognize that, compared to most consumer products, market research involving car buyers has a unique, built-in advantage — the exact names and addresses of buyers are known — and it is relatively easy to follow up on people who have bought a particular type of car or to study a group of owners of older cars who are due to come back on the market for a new model.

And GM was well on to this. Starting in 1934, they instigated what is known as the Continuing Automotive Market Information Program, which is a mail survey each year of from 80,000 to 90,000 recent new car buyers. The purpose: to continuously monitor who is buying what, why, and subsequent satisfaction. The CAMIP study continues today.

Getting back to the Falcon — naturally, GM responded; they introduced the sporty Corvair and the Chevy II, or Nova (which, incidentally, was the first body size with an "X" car designation at GM). But Ford was preparing to go a step further. In 1962, they announced plans for a 156", front-wheel-drive vehicle with a German-made engine priced at about $1,700. Code name: the Cardinal.

Later in '62, Lee Iacocca, then general manager of Ford's Ford division, announced that plans for the Cardinal were being deferred because of "the tremendous transition and changes away from economy cars." Had Ford gone ahead then, the situation could have been much different.

The Middle Years — The Monza, and Others

Back to the concern to create attractive profits on the "compact" cars — one possible solution for the Big Three was to jazz up their compacts with sporty options, all of which were very profitable to dealers.

GM's success with the Corvair Monza — with two doors, buckets, and stripes — was a key development here. It was followed by a souped-up Falcon called the Futura and an up-scale Comet called the S-22.

So, at the time, the trend in Detroit was to take the compacts and turn them into what passed for a poor man's sports car — with a larger profit potential.

The sales of Falcons, Corvairs, and other such "compacts" were a well-established fact in Detroit going into the 1960s, and judging from this statement by Marley F. Copp, assistant chief engineer at the Ford division of Ford Motor Company, the small-car situation was felt to be well in hand. Citing the advent of the Falcon in late 1959, Mr. Copp said, "We'll make anything the public wants to buy, so long as a reasonable proportion of the public wants something. That is the basis under which we are doing our long-range thinking at Ford, and I'm sure this is the promise of the future for all U.S. motor car producers."

Mr. Copp went on to credit American Motors for their "good job" and "agility" in marketing the Rambler, but warned that foreign car manufacturers will "feel our strength, too."

Be that as it may, the heartfelt convictions of Big Three top management were probably summarized in the 1960 statement of Harlow H. Curtice who had been president of GM through 1958: "I don't think the American buyer really wants a compact car — the trend will be for bigger cars." A researcher, at the time a GM employee, who made a presentation in 1962 to GM's board of directors and concluded with the recommendation that they market a car on the same wheel base as a VW Beetle, told me the reaction was "violent." Why? "Our dealers would never sit still for it."

Unsafe at Any Speed

Through the 1960s, the Big Three continued to crank out "compacts" — Pinto, Vega, Gremlin, Valiant, etc., none of which are renowned for quality engineering — but by the end of that decade, with a gallon of regular gasoline selling for about 35.7 cents, foreign imports accounted for 17 to 18 percent of new car registrations in the United States. And a new specter had arisen — consumerism, as personified by one Ralph Nader who attacked small cars, and especially GM's Corvair, as being "unsafe at any speed." This and other developments started to bring the U.S. government into Detroit's act; regulations would be soon to follow.

Detroit's interest in consumer behavior also was shifting. In 1960, GM started what was known as the Product Image and Awareness Study. Instigated by James M. Roche, who became president of GM in 1965, the original purpose was to continuously evaluate the effectiveness of GM advertising, according to Donald B. Batson, currently director/technical services at GM. This consumer research program, which was designed by a committee of research people from all of GM's advertising agencies, was assigned in 1962 to Audits & Surveys, Inc., New York. Based on 18,000 personal, in-home interviews, this PIAS program cost about $1 million a year, and it probably was the most sophisticated measure of attitudes, buying intentions, and subsequent purchasing behavior sponsored by American industry. (In the early 1970s, with the cost of in-home interviews escalating, the program switched over to telephone interviews through Amrigon, Inc., a Detroit-based research company.)

The point is: it is difficult to say Detroit didn't know what was going on in the marketplace from the ultimate consumer's point of view. But how these data were interpreted and reacted to — well, that's another subject.

Half-Hearted Response

Based on what had happened by the end of the 1960s, no one could say Detroit's Big Three had not responded to the small car market or tried, in their own way, to shut the door on foreign imports. But the imports continued to grow in popularity. Why? In retrospect, the reasons seem to be:

- American-made cars didn't compare well with imports in terms of quality construction and, in some instances, styling.

- Detroit was selling "small" per se while imports were selling economy of operation, low maintenance, and dependability.

- Importers were adventuresome marketers; witness the now famous Doyle, Dane, Bernbach campaign for Volkswagen, cited in 1980 by a panel of experts as the "outstanding advertising effort of modern times."

- Some Americans, at least, seem to perceive foreign-made products as more exotic, distinctive.

- Detroit's top management still didn't have their hearts in small car production; the return on investment wasn't there. Further, despite sales gains, the small car market was perceived as a fringe market, not the core of consumer demand.

In sum, Detroit had reacted — but not to the full extent of its capabilities.

Speaking of small cars, "The first ones we did were ugly as hell," recalls William L. Mitchell, vice president/design at GM for 19 years and now retired. From a designer's point of view, he adds, "It was hard to get excited about funny little cars, and the pressure wasn't on from management to get outstanding design. Chevette [first marketed in 1975] was the first [GM] effort to make a really good-looking small car." In Mr. Mitchell's opinion, "The designers in Europe were way ahead of us."

Another man in a position to know is Norman Krandall, now executive director, corporate strategy and analysis, at Ford Motor Company. Mr. Krandall was in product planning in the 1950s and '60s and succeeded George Brown as director of market research in 1969. At one time, he was manager of a factory that made Falcons.

"Our research interest levels were not well developed in the 1950s and '60s," Mr. Krandall told me recently, "and mostly we were sloshing around in demographics." George Brown's statements notwithstanding, Mr. Krandall feels, "Not a hell of a lot of research went into the Falcon." In those days, he recalls, "Nobody showed a model to potential customers before going to steel. We were making the cars as cheaply as we could make them."

An advertising agency executive, who prefers to be anonymous because he is still active on a GM account in Detroit, recently told me, "The quality control on those first little cars left much to be desired and, worse, some just weren't comfortable. The interiors were unattractive with cheap little door handles." In contrast, at least in his opinion, "The European cars had internal furnishings and style."

The Foreign Approach

Mr. Krandall makes another telling point, which is *Economic Fact of Life No. 4:* Foreign manufacturers have had a great cost advantage over the United States, and they could build more quality into a car. "Today [1980]," he says, "the average labor cost in Detroit is about $16 an hour, including fringes. In Japan it's $7.50 to $7.75, but when you figure in higher productivity, it's more like $6 in our terms." This same relationship existed back in the '60s, and maybe more so — and that meant the foreign cars could include more hand labor (read "quality") and still be price competitive after being shipped halfway around the world.

This was a particularly important point because it was in the late 1960s that the Japanese started to make their major moves into the U.S. market, and before long funny names like Toyota, Datsun, Subaru, Mazda, and Honda would start showing up on American TV — and in GM, Ford, and Chrysler dealerships.

The European manufacturers, exemplified by Volkswagen, had taken the tack through the 1950s and '60s of building their own dealer organizations, an expensive and laborious process, which includes brick and mortar, stockpiling of spare parts, and the training of personnel, especially service people.

The Japanese manufacturers took a different tack; they selectively sought out established Big Three dealers and convinced them to add their cars to their product line. It was variable costs all the way; there was little to lose and, as we've seen, much to gain. The Japanese auto industry, I've been told, has the capacity to produce 11 million cars a year; the Japanese home market absorbs 5 million. That leaves 6 million to sell strategically around the world. They were in a position to wheel and deal.

And this gets us to *Economic Fact of Life No. 5:* The Japanese ability to cherry pick and ride on the back of established Big Three dealerships in the United States probably, in the beginning, hurt Detroit more than any other single thing.

The huge dealer organizations — GM alone has 11,400 — had traditionally brought a great deal of stability to the U.S. car market. Because so many sales choices can be influenced at the point of sale, and because there's a certain amount of momentum from repeat business, the dealer organization could bouy up a bad model year by pushing relatively unpopular cars. So, in effect, if a division of GM made a bad style decision, the dealer organization could help carry sales through to the next model year when it could be corrected.

The Japanese modus operandi was to induce a U.S. dealership to take on their line as a sideline and then, as sales grew, to open a separate showroom nearby, featuring just the Japanese cars. So, what the public might perceive as a Datsun dealership could well be just an annex of a weak Ford dealership down the street.

So, if the Detroit product wasn't selling well and the Japanese product was, it was relatively simple to shift key personnel — and sales enthusiasm — down the street. (Ironically, this situation may today be a great help to Detroit's Big Three; some of their dealerships which might have otherwise gone under will survive because of their import sales — and hence still be alive when Detroit makes its comeback.)

The Japanese were alert in other ways, too. According to Mr. Mitchell, "Many of them had offices in Los Angeles long before; they were using the best design talent in California, especially the Arts Center College School of Design in Pasadena. Many of those Japanese cars were designed by Americans for Americans, and they didn't get sucked into the flat box look favored by the Europeans; they came in with crowned, curved looks."

Another bright move by the Japanese is to test a new model for one year in the Japanese market before bringing it into the United States. The result is an elimination of "new model bugs," which annoy consumers. According to David Power, president of J. D. Power & Associates, a Los Angeles market research company that works for both the Japanese importers and Detroit, there is a lesson to be learned from that. "Since 1972 we've interviewed [via mail] the first 1,000 buyers of almost all new model introductions in the United States. When you ask buyers, within two or three months after purchase, if they have had any problems with their new car, Omni-Horizon buyers say 'yes' about 74 percent of the time. Buyers of new cars from Mitsubishi — the Dodge Colt, Plymouth Arrow, Challenger — have a much lower rate — about 35 to 40 percent. All these cars are being sold through Chrysler Corporation dealers, of course, so that's constant, and most of the problems relate to delivery condition of the car. Generally, the U.S.-made cars are faulted much more on body work, body parts."

The OPEC Impact

A gallon of regular gasoline was selling for about 38.8 cents just before the first oil embargo in October of 1973; the price was up to 59.5 cents by 1976, and at least some Americans were starting to scream bloody murder.

And it was in this period — 1973-74 — that Detroit's Big Three started to put some muscle into their reaction to foreign imports. There are two outstanding examples of this: GM's sub-compact Chevette and Ford's Fiesta.

What is now known as the Chevette was being produced by GM through its European subsidiaries long before. When the decision was made to modify its design and to mass produce the result inside the United States, GM borrowed $600 million to cover the tooling expenses. And, as Mr. Mitchell noted earlier, "Chevette was the first effort to make a good-looking car." In any case, the Chevette was introduced in the United States on September 16, 1975.

Concurrent with this effort, Ford was going through an extensive research program, which reputedly cost $2 million, to develop a wholly new small car entry, the Fiesta, the story of which is documented in a book entitled *Let's Call It Fiesta.*

Now it is important to make the distinction between "market" research in Detroit and "styling" research, which is usually sponsored by product development people away ahead of marketing decisions.

The days in Detroit when a new car design "went to steel" before being appraised for consumer reaction had passed. GM lagged way behind Ford in this respect, but now every effort was being made at the design stage — often four years before production started — to eliminate bugs or build in features that would affect the car's sales. This was done through a laborious and expensive process called Advance Product Style Clinics. Prototypes, or mock-ups, of proposed models were made up and quite often shipped to southern California, which is believed by Detroit to be a harbinger of U.S. auto tastes.

One of the most experienced companies in this work — Rogers National Research, Inc., in Toledo, Ohio, who has worked for GM, Ford, and Chrysler — offers a good example of what happens. Say the target audience for a new design is young married couples. A group of such respondents would be recruited and brought to a showroom in the wraps of considerable secrecy to be exposed to the test car mock-up and competitive models from the world market. Every detail of the car is explored as the would-be prospects pore over it, and the results are then fed back to designers in Detroit.

Much of the $2 million spent on researching the Fiesta was for such style research, and one momentous style clinic was conducted in December of 1972 in the Palais de Beaulieu exhibit hall in Lucerne, Switzerland. Over two weeks, research companies retained by Ford flew in 700 respondents from London, Paris, Madrid, Milan, and Dusseldorf. Each separate group, through questionnaires in their own language, reacted to the proposed Fiesta design (which then had the code designation "blue car") vis-à-vis a Peugeot 104, Fiat 127, Renault 5, Honda Civic, and two mini-mites. In the United States,

Rogers National Research was conducting similar style clinics. In such a way, the Fiesta design, which was styled by Alessandro de Tomaso and included front-wheel drive, was appraised for its world sales potential and style competitiveness. Capital investment in production was estimated at $800 million.

This was the "most serious research" ever put into a new Ford car, says Mr. Krandall, "and the result is one of the best small cars in the world." Further, now that the Fiesta is on the road, "It has the best consumer acceptance rating of any Ford car," he adds. (It is interesting to note that today the Fiesta is currently advertised as "The Wundercar from Germany — a masterpiece of European engineering." Ford's market research shows that American car buyers believe that foreign-made cars are of higher quality and better design.)

Chevette and Fiesta get us to *Economic Fact of Life No. 6:* It is very time-consuming and expensive for Detroit to tool up for the production of an entirely new model car.

We've seen that the capital expenditure consequences of Chevette and Fiesta were from $600 to $800 million — and that was in the early 1970s; today, the figures would be closer to $1 billion. And such innovations as the Fiesta can be up to four years in the planning. After such a commitment is made and the car finally comes on to the market, many things can happen — and if you've planned/guessed wrong, you can end up with one very big turkey on your hands.

Detroit's top management certainly would want to be very sure of their ground before making such a major move. And it must be very frustrating to them to have outsiders ask why they don't build this or that in immediate response to the whims of the marketplace.

In fact, early research showed that the Chevette was not a good "import fighter," according to Dave Power. "Our research on the Chevette showed that it was not appealing to the kinds of people who were making the import car market," says Mr. Power. "Instead, it was appealing basically to those who were already Chevrolet customers."

At the same time, I think it is important to recognize that Detroit wasn't hurting in those days; 1972 was a near record year, 9.3 million American-made cars; 1973 was the record year for U.S.-made cars: 9.7 million. Detroit was selling all the big cars it could make.

Also, Detroit got a helping hand from Washington. President Nixon, as part of his wage and price fixing program, which started in August of 1971, put a 10 percent surcharge on imported autos (the import tax had been running at 3.5 percent). This was removed, however, in 1973, and today [1980] it runs at 2 percent.

By the mid-1970s, Americans had learned a great deal about places named Kuwait, Bahrain, Saudi Arabia, and Iran. A gallon of regular gasoline was selling for more than 63 cents. The original OPEC price increase in October 1973 had been 70 percent; the second one in December 1973 had been 130 percent. It was this second increase, according to one executive at GM, that led top management to conclude that "this is a basic change," and serious plans started to be made to downsize the standard cars.

It was also in the mid-1970s that Volkswagen abandoned the little Beetle, which had served them so well, and started to bring their sporty, second-generation cars into the United States — the Dasher in 1974, the Rabbit in '75. On April 23, 1976, they announced the decision to build an assembly plant in the U.S.

Shades of the Cardinal — it was in 1975, it has been reported, when Lee Iacocca again recommended to Ford's top management that they bankroll a small, front-wheel drive car — this time using a Honda power train. Since the commitment to Fiesta had already been made, this suggestion was rejected. According to Iacocca now, "It was the greatest tactical error in automotive history. They get an F for management."

Still, Detroit traditionalists could take heart in the fact that by 1975-76 sales of imports had started to decline; their share of new car registrations went from 18.2 percent to 14.8 percent in 1976. And this added fuel to the argument, "See, now Americans are getting back to what they've always wanted in the first place — a comfortable, standard-sized car."

The Government's Role

In 1975 Congress — convinced that oil conservation was necessary and that the Big Three were dragging their feet in the development of fuel-economy cars — passed the Energy Policy and Conservation Act, Public Law #94-163. The main stipulation was that, starting with the 1978 model year, Detroit would have to produce a line of cars that, on average, had higher miles per gallon ratings each year, ending up with 27.5 by 1985. At the time, Detroit's fleets were averaging about 13 to 14 mpg.

And this brings us to ***Economic Fact of Life No. 7:*** The federal government, just one step away from direct regulation, has had a heavy hand in Detroit's production strategies for over five years. Downsizing (to save weight), inclusion of new safety features, and the emission control regulations combined to tie up the Big Three's design time and financial resources.

Was this drastic step really necessary? Well, judging from this quote from President Jimmy Carter's news conference, as reported in *The New York Times* of April 17, 1980, the Administration thought so.

I remember the first months [1977] I was President . . . talking to the leaders of the American automobile manufacturers . . . encouraging them to comply with the impending legislation of the Congress to require the production of small and efficient automobiles for the American market.

Their unanimous reply was that this was an inappropriate thing for them to do — that the market was not there for the small and efficient automobile.

Could it really be that Detroit had yet to get (or should I say, accept) the small-car message? There's no way of knowing, of course, how accurately these brief remarks by Carter reflected all the arguments made by Detroit's leaders — but one thing was certain: making fuel-efficient cars had become the law of the land, and manufacturers who could make plastic look like steel were to have a field day.

The "pending legislation" referred to by President Carter was Public Law #95-618, the so-called "gas guzzler" tax, which stipulated that, starting with model year 1980, a surtax would be levied on autos which have a mpg rating under a specified level. Shades of George Romney!

This leads us to *Economic Fact of Life No. 8:* To meet the new economy-car production demands, Detroit itself had become a major importer of foreign-made auto parts. One reason was to save time and money. To rush the Chevette to market after the Arab oil embargo, for example, it was decided to import automatic transmissions from a GM plant in France already tooled and under-utilized. Another reason was cost and quality. A Ford study, as reported in the *Wall Street Journal* recently, indicated that a particular motor needed in the United States could be made for as little as $704, at a particular point in time, by Ford's Japanese affiliate, Toyo Kogyo. The same engine made in the U.S. would cost $1,062. In addition, to produce in the U.S. would involve tooling costs.

One result of all this, according to the *WSJ* report, is that Chrysler's Omni and Horizon get about 14 percent of their components from outside the United States, including German engines, manual front-wheel drives, transmissions, and starters.

When Ford's new compact car, the Escort, is introduced this fall [fall of 1980], the front-drive systems and steering wheels will come from Japan; other steering parts will be British-made; key front suspension parts will be Spanish; and the fuel pumps will be Italian. When Chrysler's new Ariels and Reliant compacts come on the market, the motors will be Japanese.

So, when Ford, Chrysler, and UAW executives trooped to Washington in May of 1980 to plead for some sort of restrictions on foreign-made car imports, this situation undercut their arguments for protectionism.

The need to import foreign-made components brings us to **Economic Fact of Life No. 9:** Compared to foreign auto manufacturers, U.S. production facilities are old and in need of modernization.

Of the 18 assembly plants operated by Ford in the United States, the average age is 29 years, according to a recent report in *Forbes.* Of GM's 26 domestic assembly plants, only three have been built since 1965; one, a Buick plant in Flint, Michigan, dates back to 1903. Ford's famous assembly plant at Rouge, where the public is invited to take "The Incredible Factory Tour" featured in TV commercials, was built in 1918. In contrast, many Japanese auto plants have been built within the past 10 years.

Money and technology that could have gone to modernize Detroit's plant have instead gone to support the crash programs dictated by government safety and economy regulations, argue United States auto leaders, and that hurts.

In 1979, there were additional blows from the Middle East — a new round of OPEC price increases and, in May, a cut-off of Iranian oil supplies. The need for fuel economy was more dramatic than ever.

By mid-1979, one of the Big Three — Chrysler — was on the verge of bankruptcy, and as part of a government-backed loan, the company effectively came under government control in May 1980 through the Chrysler Loan Guarantee Board, a group of Treasury Department officials. That board is now in a position to tell Lee A. Iacocca, president of Chrysler, how to market the "K" body car, which was meant to be the turnaround for the beleaguered company.

Ford's finances are in bad shape, too. The company's U.S. operations posted huge losses in the fourth quarter of 1979 and the first quarter of 1980, with more expected; only the overseas operations are profitable. By the end of 1980, the situation could be as bad as at Chrysler.

A gallon of regular gasoline now sells for $1.29, and about 27 percent of the new cars and trucks sold in the United States are imports. The only bright spot in Detroit is the "X" car sales, limited only by production capacity. And, Jimmy Carter, if anything, is now figuring out how to help our crippled auto industry, and he'll probably come up with something simply because it's an election year.

As this article has attempted to point out, it has taken a long time for Detroit to get into this mess, and it is apt to take a long time to get out; the bleak economic facts of life with which Detroit must cope still exist. And no one is apt to argue with this prediction made by Lee Iacocca in late May 1980: "The next six months to a year are going to be pure hell."

Chapter 3

Launching Renault's Alliance

After years of gloom and doom in the U.S. automobile industry, a really upbeat marketing effort took place starting September 22, 1982. Two most unlikely partners — American Motors Corporation and Régie Nationale des Usines Renault, the French auto manufacturer — teamed up to market a little subcompact called the Alliance in the United States. The success of this launch gave AMC a new lease on life, and, perhaps more important, it showed Detroit that a really well-made car, at a reasonable price, will sell as well as the imports, despite a relatively weak dealer network.

W. Paul Tippett, Jr., chairman of AMC, gave me almost complete access to his organization and its consumer / marketing research files — and much of the article (which appeared in Advertising Age *June 6, 1983) is based on information that had never been published before.*

Of special interest is the candid interview with Mr. Tippett, some of which did not appear in Advertising Age *due to space limitations. As you'll see, he is a very flat-out man.*

The Alliance Story

Is a little 56-hp. car designed in France powerful enough to haul one of America's largest corporations out of its deep financial ditch?

Given that the car is Renault's Alliance and the corporation is American Motors, the answer at this point of time [1983] is a hopeful "yes." United States and Canadian sales of this much-acclaimed, front-wheel drive subcompact are expected to exceed 140,000 units during its first 12 months on the market (October '82 — September '83), despite a 1.3 percent price increase in April 1983.

The significance of this consumer endorsement to AMC, which lost $491 million over the three years 1980-82; to Renault, who has been trying to dent the U.S. auto market since 1904; and to 10,800 auto workers in Kenosha, Wisconsin, where the Alliance is manufactured, is almost beyond measure. As for AMC's dealer network, Nat

Ross, the happy sales manager of Tappan Motors, Inc., which has been representing AMC products in North Tarrytown, N.Y., for 22 years, recently told me, "The Alliance is a franchise all its own."

What follows is an insider's story of the $13.5 million marketing program behind the Alliance's successful U.S. launch, which AMC people consider "one of the smoothest in Detroit's history."

This story, written with the blessing of AMC's top management, dates back to 1977. It details the $1 million consumer research program that guided the Alliance's market positioning and copy strategy, the creative contest between AMC's agencies, Grey and Compton, for "the copy" that would introduce the Alliance, the media strategy, and the "Get to know Renault . . ." program that was felt necessary to convince old-time AMC dealers that the Renault name, considered a liability by many, could be transformed into a marketing plus.

And, maybe above all, it highlights the hands-on insistence of José J. Dedeurwaerder, the Renault manufacturing executive who joined AMC in 1981 and became president in January '82, that the Alliance — which, after all, is the star of this saga — has construction quality equal to, or better than, comparable Japanese-made cars. (*Motor Trend* magazine, in naming the Alliance "Car of the Year" for 1983, said, "It may well be the best assembled first-year car we've ever seen.")

Born of Necessity

The Alliance might be viewed as a child born of a mixed marriage, an automotive marriage of convenience. Courtship started in 1977 when AMC's top management, led by Gerald C. Meyers (chairman from 1978 to January '82, now retired), concluded that to survive in the U.S. market, the company "had to acquire advanced technology quickly and at minimum cost."

AMC's auto products in those days were "off the same platform," as they say in Detroitese when spin-offs of the same basic design are presented to the public, after some cosmetic, or shell, alterations, as different cars. The AMC Concord, for instance, was a variation of the Hornet, and the Spirit was a revamped Gremlin. "We had changed the skirts on the old girl as much as we could; we needed something really new," says Robert Schwartz, vp, North American sales, at AMC from 1982 to January '83.

This situation led to exploratory talks with several auto makers, both in Europe and Japan, but AMC's urgent needs seemed to mesh most naturally with those of Régie Nationale des Usines Renault, the world's sixth largest auto manufacturer, which is owned by the French government.

In the spring of '78, AMC and Renault started to deal seriously, and about nine months later they signed an agreement that called for

AMC to become the exclusive importer and distributor of Renault-made autos in the United States and Canada. (This was overshadowed at the time by Chrysler's way out of a similar bind — the controversial, government-backed survival loan of $1.2 billion.)

The lure to Renault was AMC's dealer organization (Renault calls them "stores"), which numbered about 1,350 at the time. It was, by Ford or General Motors standards,a hodgepodge; some AMC dealers had a strong Jeep orientation; some carried only AMC products; others had had some Renault product experience. Many were relatively small "stores" off of auto row, and as Mr. Schwartz observed recently, "Their one distinguishing factor was that they were survivors of the hard times at AMC," dealers who had stayed alive by pushing their service department and/or used car sales, or by taking on one or more competitive lines. (Mr. Ross's dealership in North Tarrytown, for instance, handles Mazda, Jaguar, and Dodge's Omni in addition to Jeep and other AMC cars.)

Because of the AMC-Renault agreement, two Renault-made cars were pushed into AMC's dealer network: the mini-compact LeCar and a larger subcompact called the "18i," a blah car with little sales appeal.

Need to Sell Dealers

Dealer enthusiasm for the Renault-AMC pact, the Renault name, and Renault-made products was well under control; in fact, the negative feelings threatened to undermine the long-range plans to launch the Alliance in the United States. As many sales/marketing managers have learned the hard way, sometimes the really hard sell is not the consumer — it's one's own organization.

This problem was on the table, up front, says Mr. Schwartz, who made a presentation to Renault's board regarding what he thought to be the need for special efforts (and expenditures) to win the dealers over to Renault identification with the new (as yet unnamed) car that would become the Alliance, and to convince U.S. consumers that it was a departure from Renault's lackluster past in the U.S. auto market (1959 was the peak — 91,900 units, two-thirds of which were Dauphines, which it takes a real auto buff to remember). "The French understood," adds Mr. Schwartz. (One reason may be that, previously, Renault had retained the management consulting firm of Hoagland & MacLachlan & Company in Wellesley, Massachusetts, to survey AMC dealers.)

In 1979, knowing that a new car (as yet undescribed) was coming, the AMC Dealer Advisory Board voted unanimously against giving it Renault's name, says Mr. Schwartz, and, "They would have been in absolute revolt if we didn't do something." The "something" turned out to be a "Get to know Renault. . ." road show that started with dealers in the Boston area in March '81. Eventually, this upbeat presentation about Renault's prowess in the European auto market was taken to 30 markets. One result was that about a year later, when the advisory board was told of upcoming plans for the Alliance and the use of Renault's name, no member objected.

The X-42

During the "Get to know Renault. . ." campaign, AMC dealers knew more Renault cars were coming their way, but they didn't know exactly what. Internally, at AMC's headquarters in Southfield, Michigan, executives referred to the car that would be the Alliance by the code name X-42, but only a handful knew that it would be an Americanized version of a Renault car called the R-9, a subcompact designed to compete in what is known in Europe as the "Class 3, small" category.

Built in Renault's new plant in Douai, France, considered one of the finest production facilities in Europe, the R-9 has since become the second best selling car in Europe and the best seller in France. It was named Europe's Car of the Year in 1982.

The man in charge of production at Douai and credited with the R-9's quality was José J. Dedeurwaerder, who joined AMC as executive vice president in September 1981 to oversee production of the Alliance.

Modifications of the R-9 for the U.S. market included a fuel injection system (to make it peppier), a fancier interior, different headlights and antenna, extended bumpers, a softer suspension, and a two-door model. The car was destined for a market segment Detroit refers to as "subcompact, standard" — which accounts for about 23 percent of U.S. auto sales in units; it's the guts of the current market. There are 24 name plates in this category, some of the most prominent being Plymouth's Horizon, Honda's Civic, Toyota's Corolla, Chevrolet's Chevette, and the best seller — by far — Ford's Escort. About 80 percent of these subcompact cars are purchased as the "primary car," according to AMC research; the balance are viewed as second cars.

This is considered to be an especially price-sensitive segment of the market, and right from the start one of AMC's marketing goals was to give the Alliance a very competitive — you might say "low ball" — price; the basic two-door model, stripped, had a sticker price of $5,595, which was featured in advertising. "Research showed we could have started with a higher price," says David J. Van Peursem, general manager/marketing, at AMC, "but it was a marketing decision to keep it low; we wanted everything going for us, considering the importance of this launch." (The model MT, which is the fully loaded configuration tested by *Motor Trend*, had a sticker price of $9,200.)

Naming the Baby

The consumer research program, which had much to do in defining the qualitative positioning of the Alliance and which eventually cost about $1 million, started in the summer of '79, three full years before Alliance Announcement Day (to the general public) on September 22, 1982. There were two key players: David G. Garfield, manager/marketing services, at AMC, and Joseph G. Smith, president of the New York-based survey research firm of Oxtoby-Smith, Inc., which since 1972 has, under retainer, provided about 85 percent of AMC's custom research work.

"We were trying to figure out how to sell the car [X-42], and we didn't know what we didn't know," recalls Mr. Garfield. There were several key questions, such as, "What does 'European' mean?" [to U.S. consumers]; "what does 'Renault' or 'imported' mean?" Exploration of these and related questions was the purpose of six focus-group interviews, and shortly after, in August, the first auto clinic was conducted in Anaheim, California.

Such "clinics" are commonplace in auto marketing. You rent a showroom and recruit a group of people who are typical of the target group "the car" is aimed at (in the case of the X-42, buyers of compacts, young, relatively well-educated, and import-car oriented). These people are then allowed to inspect closely, at leisure, a mock-up, or prototype, or real-thing model of "the car," which might be displayed along with other cars that are directly competitive, with or without identifying name plates. ("Over half of the people can't recognize the cars after the name plates are taken off," says Mr. Garfield.)

The first clinic used a fiberglass mock-up since there were no R-9s then, and focused on exterior-only properties. A second clinic in San Mateo, California, in April, had three sessions; each presented a prototype in a different light — as a Renault product, as an AMC product, or as a "no name." The key findings: The car itself got positive scores, but these were less positive when the car had a Renault identification. The same was true with an AMC identification, but less so. (This clinic also included mock-ups of the new Renault car, code name X-37, which might be considered competitive to the X-42.)

Meanwhile, the question of name was on the table. "About 1,000 were suggested by management, our agencies, suppliers — everyone," says Mr. Garfield. These were reduced, judgmentally, to 10 finalists, and consumer research was done to establish the imagery inherent in each because, according to Mr. Garfield, one of the goals was to match the car's image with a name that reinforced that image.

The research, which was done by Burke Marketing Research, produced "Alliance," and the only concern was prior claim to the name. (The closest one that could be identified was a tire manufacturer in Israel.) "American" was the runner-up name, and some also-rans were "Radiant," "Pioneer," and "Resolute."

A third series of clinics took place in Long Beach, California, in July of '81. Now one of the descriptors could be "Renault Alliance" — the first time the name was used. Respondents at the clinics were interviewed, prior to seeing the cars, as to what car they would be most apt to shop for and buy, given that they were in the market. A comparable interview afterwards provided a measure of the Alliance's ability to "switch off" buyers interested in competitive cars. The Alliance's attraction power was established.

Also going on in the fall of '81 were focus-group sessions designed to develop hypotheses for a full-scale survey to determine "how best to position the Alliance in the American marketplace in order to maximize its chances of success."

Based on face-to-face interviews with 605 respondents in eight cities (mall intercepts), this study was fielded in January-February '82. Respondents were shown pictures of the Alliance and told of its performance characteristics, and these were pitted against the Escort, Civic, Horizon, and Mazda's GLC. Three "genealogies" were presented: the Alliance was a car (1) of Renault origin, (2) of joint AMC/Renault origin, and (3) of AMC origin. Also measured was the relative importance of stressing quality, technology, or durability. One of the study's key findings, and I quote from Oxtoby-Smith's report:

> Purchase interest in the Alliance, regardless of which genealogy was revealed, was much more favorable than predisposition to Renault and AMC generally. Indeed, the car overcame relatively unfavorable predispositions to each manufacturer.

Other conclusions from the study were: "There was a distinct edge for the Renault genealogy in generating strong purchase interest in the Alliance, and 'Made in America' was much more frequently mentioned as a reason for strong purchase interest . . . among those exposed to the mixed and AMC genealogies." Also, "Respondents clearly found the durability and technology positionings more attractive . . . ," especially among key target groups (young, more upscale, import prospects). The decision was made to emphasize "technology," partly because "durability" proof was down the road, too early to substantiate. "The question now was how to talk about 'technology,'" recalls Mr. Garfield, "because buyers were more results-oriented than process-oriented."

Beyond the analytical researcher concerns about the best name or positioning of the X-42, you can well imagine that there were strong undercurrents of opinions fueled by the pride of two pioneer auto manufacturers, both hungry for a winner. Beyond pride was the fact that Renault started in 1979 to acquire AMC stock, and by December '80, its ownership equity had reached 46.4 percent.

Since 1979 Renault has, in effect, served as AMC's banker, and that facilitated the election of Mr. Dedeurwaerder as president and COO — and, in essence, Mr. Quality Control — in January '82. At the same time, W. Paul Tippett, Jr., who had joined AMC as president in 1978, was elected chairman of the board and CEO.

The Advertising Battle — Grey vs. Compton

Because of the extreme importance of getting the best possible creative to launch the Alliance, Mr. Van Peursem did something that may be a "first" for Detroit; he asked both of AMC's agencies (Grey Advertising on autos and Compton Advertising on Jeep products) to prepare creative for consideration. But, no matter which agency won, it was understood that the media planning and billing would be through Grey. How did that go over? "Compton was delighted," recalls Mr. Van Peursem, "but Grey was a little thunderstruck — until I explained the reasoning behind the decision. And, after all, it's reciprocal; Grey is now helping with advertising on our new Jeep line."

Both agencies maintain offices in AMC's 25-story headquarters building, American Center, in Southfield, but they quickly turned to their home offices in New York for creative help. A batch of focus-group sessions were done for guidance, some paid for by AMC, some by the agencies. The result was about 50 storyboards, four of which were converted into animatics (photographing a series of drawings with sound track for testing). These were "Chasm" and "Plastic Car" from Grey and "Way to Go, Renault" and "Love It" from Compton.

Evaluation was done through a pre-testing methodology — which emphasizes persuasion measures — developed by Oxtoby-Smith. Respondents recruited in mall intercepts were shown double exposures of the copy within a TV pilot film context.

Three of the commercials had virtually the same scores, according to Joseph E. Cappy, a former Ford executive who joined AMC as vice president/marketing group in 1982. "We leaned towards going with 'Plastic Car,' but production time was estimated to be long and production costs too high, so we went with 'Chasm'," says Mr. Cappy.

"Chasm" pictures two land masses converging; one represents European technology and styling and the other affordability. When they come together, you had the Alliance proposition. (Mr. Cappy declined to comment, but agency sources estimate the production cost for "Chasm" to be over $700,000, a number that reportedly sent shock waves through AMC's executive suite when the bills started to come in.)

But when the finished copy on "Chasm" was tested on-air in Burke's DAR system, a not-so-funny thing happened — it got a lower score than norms from other AMC commercials tested through the years. You gotta believe a lot of people wanted to know, "How come?"

So, Oxtoby-Smith was asked to put finished "Chasm" copy through its pre-test system; sure enough, it received a lower score than the original animatic test. "But," says Donald E. Payne, senior vice president/research at Oxtoby-Smith, "we went a step further; after the normal test, we exposed respondents to the original animatic and then questioned them about differences they perceived." The result was that while both finished version and animatic communicated the same message, respondents didn't like the announcer's voice or music in the finished version as much as they did in the animatic. Also, the color in the finished version seemed pale compared to that in the animatic.

Grey redid the sound track, putting back in the original announcer and music (Handel's "Water Music"), and the end result is what went on air.

Robots in Kenosha

Kenosha, Wisconsin, population about 126,000, is located on Lake Michigan about half-way between Chicago and Milwaukee. To say that AMC has deep roots there is an understatement; the first Rambler, a one-cylinder auto that sold for $750, was manufactured there in 1902 by a predecessor company, Thomas B. Jeffery Company (which in 1916 became Nash Motors; in 1937, Nash-Kelvinator; and in 1954, American Motors). That original plant — called Main Plant — is where final assembly work is being done on the Alliance today.

About 1¼ miles away, in a plant called Lakefront, which was a Simmons Mattress Company plant until AMC bought it in 1958, the Alliance bodies are framed, painted, and trimmed with the help of 24 robot welders, some manufactured by Renault, some by the Japanese. Of the $200 million that has been spent to make the Alliance's production in the United States as good as the R-9's in Douai, France, most has gone into Lakefront — including an $11 million paint system that features an electrodeposition priming process that literally adheres a protective coating to the body. The system also provides for clear-coating of metallic colors. (This shiny outer coat of colorless acrylic enamel really dresses up the Alliance vis-à-vis other cars in the same price class.) The Alliance is 75 percent domestic made (U.S. and Canada), with the power train — engine and transmission — coming in from France.

The first pilot Alliance rolled off the line at Main in January '82, the first of four pilot car runs of about 100 cars each — with a month shutdown in between — to make sure quality was satisfactory before starting production line volume. Many of these cars were given to employees for evaluation, a common practice in Detroit. But with the Alliance, there was a twist — it wasn't just top executives who got the cars; they went down into the ranks, and everyone had to fill out a performance questionnaire every week, noting any problems.

The first production model Alliance came off-line on June 18, 1982, and nearly 10,000 were produced and shipped to dealers before Announcement Day on September 22.

With a modern factory up and going and product available for review, the stage was set for another important step in the campaign to sell AMC's dealers on the Renault association. In mid-July '82 about 1,000 AMC dealers (some with sales managers, some with wives, some with both) were brought to an intensive program at the former Playboy Club resort in Lake Geneva, Wisconsin, about 60 minutes from the Kenosha plant.

"We got them right off the plane at O'Hare," recalls Mr. Van Peursem, "onto buses equipped with TV sets. We started showing films about the Alliance [the first time, officially, that the dealers were told the car's name would be Renault's Alliance] and the marketing plan. They watched this stuff on the ride up to Lake Geneva." There followed a showbiz kickoff dinner, tours of the Kenosha plant, and test drives of the Alliance at AMC's testing grounds at Burlington, Wisconsin.

As for the Alliance's quality, Mr. Schwartz says the Lake Geneva meetings proved to the dealers "that this time it's not just hype; it's true that we have a great car." The Renault issue was fading.

Task Force

In February of '82, introduction plans — complete with time sequencing diagrams — started to build up steam. First, there was an X-42 Task Force created with all functions — public relations, sales training, merchandising, service, dealer advertising, market planning, etc. — represented with a member. It was the sole responsibility of the task force manager, William R. Chapin, to pull it all together and expedite its activities. (Mr. Chapin is the son of Roy D. Chapin, Jr., a former chairman of AMC, and a grandson of Roy D. Chapin,

Sr., one of the founders of Hudson Motor Car Company.) This task force reported — weekly, towards the end — to a top management review committee that okayed major moves.

As for communications, the budget was divided generally as follows: 70 percent to advertising in measured media, 10 percent for merchandising materials (dealer kits, point of sale, etc.), 10 percent for public relations, and 10 percent for miscellaneous matters such as shows, meetings, etc.

The national advertising plan, according to Howard I. Mosher, director of Renault marketing at AMC, called for 70 percent of the budget going into broad-reach TV network, with participation in special events as much as possible. (The first Alliance commercial on-air was on September 13, a week prior to Announcement Day; that was due to an opening on the U.S. Open tennis tournament telecast.) The plan called for 200 to 300 gross rating points per week during the first four-week flight and a 150-point average each week in the balance of the introductory period.

Grey had developed a pool of four commercials, two :60s and two :30s, for the introduction. "We felt the :60s were important," asserts Mr. Cappy, "because the Alliance is not a car with just one outstanding feature; instead it rates very high on a lot of features. When you can tell that whole story, testing showed that people said, 'I'd better have a look at that car.'"

The 200 AMC dealer associations were offered 25-second versions with room for an identification tag. "We urged the associations to use our copy to tie in with the total campaign," says Mr. Van Peursem, "and most of them cooperated." The factory picked up 45 percent of the air time costs.

On the public relations front, AMC tried an innovation that may also have been a first for Detroit, according to John G. McCandless, manager/sales and marketing communications. "The idea was to tie in with local public relations firms, just like co-op advertising, with the hope that they — with their knowledge of the market — could create more effective media events than we could dream up from Detroit." This concept was tested in four markets, in conjunction with the local dealer associations, and then expanded to 20 markets. This worked so well, says Mr. McCandless, that the network will be used again in new auto launches next fall.

Announcement Day

Everything came together on August 29, 1982, with a National Press Review in three cities and, finally, Announcement Day to the general public on September 22. AMC's PR department had arranged for about 100 Alliances to be spotted around the country for test driving by local automobile news writers, and dealer showrooms were stocked with about a 20-day supply of Alliances (compared to an industry norm of a 50 to 60-day supply), with special emphasis on the top 200 AMC dealers, who account for about 80 percent of sales.

Nervous, "How's it going?" questions were being answered by a number of feedback devices. One is the weekly UPS (for "dealer write-ups") report at AMC, in which dealers record store traffic (limited to prospective buyers who register; i.e., give their name and address). Another is a weekly sales report from a panel of 250 key, especially large dealers.

Research fielded by Mr. Garfield in Detroit included such things as the Monitor Survey (mail survey of Alliance buyers asking, among other things, how they came to know of the car), and in the case of the Alliance, a showroom shoppers' study, done by Marketing Strategy, Inc., a research firm located in Southfield, to determine what kind of people were being drawn in to see the new Alliance.

And, finally, there is the so-called "Rejecter's Study," where known visitors to AMC showrooms are interviewed about four or five weeks later to determine what they ultimately did, and if they decided not to buy an Alliance, "Why not?" "What we found," says Mr. Garfield, "was that sometimes the car did better than the dealers; the young, educated buyers we were appealing to now often know more about cars than the floor salesman."

All systems were indicating a good response, and generally dealers were happy although some experienced a shortage of the lower priced two-door models. "I never expected it would take off like it did," says Mr. Ross, the AMC dealer in North Tarrytown; "the test drive does it." Another dealer, Vincent A. Soccodato, general manager of Biltmore AMC-Jeep-Renault in Rye, New York, was especially pleased, he told me, that the Alliance brought a different kind of buyer into his showroom. (AMC's internal research shows that 90 percent of all Alliance buyers are new to AMC.)

Marketplace feedback indicated two things: (1) In the beginning, Alliance sales took off most quickly with dealers in the north central part of the United States (and especially in southern Wisconsin, spurred by AMC employee families anxious to support the company), and (2) the "made in America" appeal of the Alliance was especially strong. Consequently, Alliance advertising was modified (revising commercial sound track) to reflect that, and in addition, "Made in America" bumper stickers and window decals were made up and rushed to dealers to put on the cars.

At a press conference in Los Angeles, California, on January 10, 1983 — just about four months after its introduction — promotional lightning struck the Alliance; *Motor Trend* magazine named it "Car of the Year" for 1983.

AMC's public relations department knew this was coming two months before and had set up a press campaign to exploit the most welcome endorsement, which — as Mr. Mosher puts it, "gave the Alliance credibility." The day after the announcement, four teams of AMC executives, headed by chairman Paul Tippett, fanned out for press conferences in 23 cities in four days. New bumper stickers and window stickers with "Car of the Year" were on hand in dealer showrooms to affix on cars.

Getting a clear-cut fix on just exactly what the *Motor Trend* award does for the sale of a car is difficult, and that is especially so with the Alliance; as luck would have it, AMC had just announced a new 11.9 percent financing plan at the same time, and how can you separate the impact of the two?

In any case, here's an indication of what happened based on weekly sales reports from a panel of 250 AMC dealers: During the best week in September, these 250 dealers sold 791 Alliances. In October, the comparable number was 1,126, and in November, 1,115. The best week in December was 870. Then, in January, in the two weeks immediately prior to the *Motor Trend* announcement, the numbers were 573 and 829. In the third week of January, immediately after the *Motor Trend* announcement, the number was 1,022, and in the week after, 1,233. The best week in February was 1,554 units.

"Half of the people who come in here," says AMC's Rye dealer, Vincent Soccodato, "don't know about *Motor Trend*," but he estimates store traffic quadrupled. "But, I don't think we'll see the full effect until after April 15 when the spring buying season starts," he adds. "Our traffic doubled," estimates Al Kilduff, co-owner of Kilduff Motors, Inc., a long-time AMC dealer in Edgewood, Maryland. "But you have to remember, a lot of magazines were saying good things about the Alliance at the same time." Most important of all, perhaps, was the huge amount of publicity the Alliance got from newspaper auto writers because of the award, and AMC's PR department has books full of clippings to show.

One of the key questions has been, "To what degree has the Alliance's prominence and success enhanced the image of both AMC and Renault to potential car buyers?" The results of an image study fielded in February 1983, suggest that progress is being made, according to Stu Lahn, senior vice president of Oxtoby-Smith, who conducted the study. "The percentage of people who would give positive purchase consideration to Renault has increased 23 percent over the levels in the last study in December 1981," he said, "and we've also seen significant increases in the positive opinions of both Renault cars and dealers."

Aftermath

The success of the Alliance's launch, with a marketing budget of $13.5 million and a dealer organization of 1,350, unfortunately cannot be compared exactly with those of Ford's Escort and Lynx, which reportedly cost $40 million, or the $20 million spent on the Horizon. In terms of dealer strength, Chevrolet's Chevette had about 6,000 — over four times the number of AMC dealers. But what is known does seem to confirm that, pound for pound, AMC's launch was, indeed, one of the most effective Detroit has seen for a long, long time.

Perhaps equally important in the long run, the Alliance's success has enabled AMC to beef up its dealer organization, which was the main lure to Renault in the first place. "For several years," says Jacque O. Polan, manager of AMC's New York Zone office in Elmsford, New York, "we were just trying to hold the organization together. About 18 months ago, we started to change all our franchising habits. For instance, now we can be more demanding about adequate training and financing. There was a time when we let a dual dealer take on our cars just to get the exposure, but now when they come around trying to get the Alliance, we can insist on a separate showroom."

That may be — aside from profits — the most important bottom line on what the Alliance means to American Motors.

W. Paul Tippett, Jr., Talks about the Alliance

W. Paul Tippett, Jr., 50, joined AMC as president, chief operating officer, and a director in 1978; in January 1982, he was elected chairman of the board and chief executive officer.

In addition to about 20 years experience in the auto industry (Ford and Lincoln-Mercury divisions of Ford, director of sales and marketing for Ford of Europe, Inc.), Mr. Tippett may well be the only top auto executive with experience in high-velocity package goods marketing. He started with Procter & Gamble as a brand manager and advertising supervisor, and at one time was executive vice president of STP Corporation.

I talked with Mr. Tippett in his office in Southfield, Michigan, on April 14, 1983. Mr. Tippett was in a good mood; AMC's first public stock offering since 1972 had been snapped up by investors the day before.

Text of April 14, 1983 Interview
with W. Paul Tippett, Jr.

Honomichl: How does it feel to have the press come to badger you to talk about the Alliance?

Tippett: It feels good. I've been rich and I've been poor, and believe me, rich is better. Not an original line, admittedly. Nevertheless, it's been a long, dry spell. We've been sitting here being beaten about the head and shoulders to death by X cars, J cars, K cars, Japanese cars, and without anything to fight back with. Now we've got something, and we've got a lot more coming — that's the important thing.

I think the marketing guys have done a great job with the product. But, as you know — you've done a lot of these stories — marketing can only accelerate the success of a product; it can't substitute for the product. If you market it well, you'll get successful faster.

My first employer was P&G, and everybody talks about what a great marketing-oriented company it is. I say, "You've got it all wrong; it really is a product-oriented company." They work so hard to bring out a better-than-average product; then they do market it well. But the few times they have tried to market a parity, or me-too product, they have fallen on their asses just like everybody else.

Honomichl: You are probably the only top executive in the auto industry who knows what high-velocity package goods are all about, with your Procter and STP background. How much of what you learned in the package goods business have you been able to infuse into the marketing of a car like the Alliance?

Tippett: A lot, of course. The principles are certainly the same. You'd better have a product that is at least as good as the competition in most areas, and better than the competition in some key areas. That's to me a principle of good package goods marketing. When you try to come out with a parity product — especially when you are the last guy in, as we were with the Alliance — you've got a lot of trouble; I don't care how good you are, how much you spend.

I've worked in Detroit for a long time — 20 years. When I first got here, a car was developed and, like six months before it was scheduled to be launched, the marketing boys were brought in and told, "Here it is; go sell it." In those days you could do that. When we started with the Alliance three, four years ago — it was not just me, it was everybody in the company — we took the attitude, which I strongly believe in, we had better design into the product things that will make it easy to market and give us some advantages, demonstrable advantages, or else we're going to have trouble.

Honomichl: What would have happened if the Alliance had bombed?

Tippett: It would not be nearly as much fun to be at the office today, Jack.

Honomichl: Would it have been the end of American Motors?

Tippett: I don't think it would have been the end of American Motors; I don't think it was that desparate. We just had a stock issue...

Honomichl: I read about it; it went out very well.

Tippett: Yes. We just sold $134 million worth of stock. We just got our banks to increase their lines with us $80 million in spite of the fact we said we were going to sell the single biggest asset we have, AM General. So, not only did we ask them for more money, we said, "By the way, the collateral is going to disappear." That's not an easy sell. So, that's $134 and $80 — $214 million. If the Alliance had not been a success, I suspect that neither one of those events would have occurred.

People said, "Can you guys do it? Can you build a new car that is of high quality and technologically superior, and if you can build it...?" They didn't say it that charitably. Most people said first, "You can't build a decent car, and even if you did, you couldn't sell it with all those red-neck dealers you've got."

Honomichl: How many big banks want to come and have lunch with you at the Detroit Club now when they wouldn't even talk with you two years ago?

Tippett: Of the $80 million we just got, $50 million was from our present banks and $30 million was from guys saying, "We'd like to loan you some money." [An aside, with hand cupped to mouth: "Where were you when I needed you?"]

We would not have gone under. I think we could have taken a longer-range view. But I think everybody — there's no question about the fact — was watching this car to see if we could make a good car and sell it in volume.

We have now proved we could do so. We are going to do it again this summer with another car. We are going to do it this fall with a new Jeep. We've done the same thing with these products. The Jeep has six or seven very important product advantages over its competition built in, which we worried about four years ago — not six months. That, to me, is what marketing is all about. I don't care how good a marketer you are, if the product isn't better — and again, if you're the last guy in like we were with the Alliance — you don't have enough money.

Obviously, there's luck involved in anything. We took a marketing viewpoint on this vehicle to begin with. Now pricing is another thing. We knew we'd have to have an advantage going in; nobody is waiting for another new car...

Honomichl: You low-balled the Alliance, didn't you?

Tippett: No, we did not low-ball it. Well, that depends on how you define it. To me, there are two ways to get a product or marketing advantage. One is "same product, lower price." The other is "better product, same price." So, we chose the "better product, same price" route. If you adjust for equipment, we are pricing right at, or now over, the Escort, which is the biggest selling car in this class. But we've got the better product. Now, if that is low-balling — maybe it is, but I don't think it is; we don't think our costs are any higher than the Escort — we think we have designed a better product and we've priced it right on them. So people say, "Gee, that's a helluva buy."

To me, that's obviously not only the better but the cheaper way to get an advantage. If you take $100 off the price of the product, that costs you $100. But if you've got $100 of value in the product, that costs us, say, $50.

So, we're not low-ball. We just raised the price by $100 last week. We started with a very competitive price on Escort, and now we're going to start moving it up a bit.

Honomichl: How many units do you have to sell a year to get into the black on the Alliance?

Tippett: Gee, that's almost an impossible question to answer; it depends upon how you allocate the costs. Ford says they are losing money on the Escort. I don't know how they calculate that. The ultimate test — whenever they say they are losing money, then the corollary of that is, "You'd make more money if you stop selling it." Is that right? Most people are not willing to go that far with you, and that's the ultimate test. Would Ford be making more money now if they stopped selling the Escort? I think the answer is "no." It would really be in the soup; the Escort absorbs a huge amount of overhead. From what we know, our costs are generally competitive with what it costs other people to make this size and kind of vehicle, and we're selling it for the same as, or more than, what they are selling for, so it's reasonably profitable for us. I tell you, I would not want to be sitting here today without the Alliance.

Honomichl: In digging into your marketing affairs, I found several innovative things. But one, because of my research background, was especially interesting: that is your making a deal with an outside research company to do most, if not all, of your consumer research. How does that work?

Tippett: Well, it seems to work out all right. Joe Smith has been with us long enough so that he has some perspective, and yet he's far enough away from us so that he can say, "Hey, you guys, that may sell well in Detroit, but it's not going to sell anywhere else."

This is a somewhat incestuous community, and we have to guard against becoming typical Detroiters. As the fourth guy in town, we can't do what the others do. We've got to be different, not peculiar different, but aggressive different, and — hopefully — imaginatively different. We've got to be right. General Motors can survive —

maybe even prosper — after the J car debacle, which that really was. They overpriced it and underpowered it. As you correctly pointed out, we would have had a lot more trouble surviving an Alliance debacle. We couldn't afford it; we have to be right every time. We have to be right with the X-37 [named Renault Encore] this summer, and I think we will be. We have to be right with the new Jeep line. We've got to build ourselves up to the point where we can afford a mistake.

Honomichl: Does that mean that you have to pay more attention to consumer research than they might?

Tippett: I think so. Every time — every single time — we've ignored it, for reasons that seemed convenient at the time, we've lived to regret it. The Alliance cliniced fantastically well; it's been successful. The Eagle cliniced well. We've done some other things that didn't clinic as well, but we said, "Well, what the hell, we like it." And we went ahead and tried it, and guess what . . . the research was right and we weren't. We ignore it at our peril. We just don't have enough clout to jam it down their throats — and I don't think anyone does any more. There's just too much choice.

Honomichl: If you could do it all over again — in retrospect — what would you do differently in marketing the Alliance? Was there something you'd do more of, or less of, or whatever?

Tippett: All I can tell you is that we're using the same checklist with the X-37 as with the Alliance. I think most things we did were right.

Oh, yeah — I'll tell you one thing — PR guys never did get the preferred view of the car in their press kits. That's one thing we'd do right next time around.

Honomichl: Are cars like actors who want to be photographed from one angle?

Tippett: Seriously, I am a nut about this. Twelve to 14 months before we launched that thing, we got professional photographers in and photographed that car from maybe 125 angles — up, down, high, low — and we looked at the transparencies, and everybody gets into it, and we finally conclude the car looks best from this precise angle. Maybe the rear end is a little weaker than the front, or the side view is stronger than . . . And then there might be two secondary views. But then I don't want to see any pictures of the car — television, print, whatever — that don't use those views; because they're like an actor, or anything else, cars are very funny things. They can look fat, they can look skinny, and they can look big or small, and if you don't get the right view . . . There is one view that optimizes things. Same with colors.

For reasons that aren't entirely clear, we never did get the PR guys totally in sync with the marketing guys.

We probably spent a little too much money advertising, but on the other hand, no one seems to know exactly what's the precise amount.

It's great now, sitting here feeling euphoric. But knowing what was riding on this car, we started production at 300 cars a day, but we wanted to get to 600 a day because there is considerable lead time. I remember this very clearly: José Dedeurwaerder, the president, and I sat in that room there and said, "We haven't sold car one to a customer, but we've had our dealer announcement shows and the dealers loved it, had the press in and they liked it," and José said to me, "If you really want to not run out of cars, we've got to make a decision by August 14 to go to a second shift." That meant hiring 2,000 people in Kenosha so we could start to build 600 cars a day in the middle of September; it takes about a month, five weeks lead time. We had to order parts, the engine and transmission, from France.

Renault said, "Do you guys know what you're doing?" I said, "No, we're not sure, obviously, but we think we ought to go; the worst thing would be to run out of cars." So, before we'd sold one car, we decided to double production — and it turned out to be the right decision. We went to 600, then to 660, and then today to 860. We didn't go up any faster because we wanted to keep the quality; one of the things that is selling this car is quality.

I really sweated that. One thing we didn't want to do — that is get into the launch and then have to put in rebates or something like that, like our competitors do. Another was to cut production; we knew that would be the worst possible thing we could do for the momentum, success feeling, image, and all that. Remember, the market was lousy then; we launched this thing in a downturn market.

On the other hand, we didn't want to run out of cars. We were spending one hundred zillion, trillion dollars on advertising. So, the famous SWAG — Scientific Wild Ass Guess; we said, "Let's put on the second shift."

Chapter 4

The Marketing
of Cycle Dog Food

Behind the facade of slick advertising, huge promotional budgets, and what appears to be the sound positioning of a consumer product, there is often a much less estimable story. Obviously, these are the stories that seldom become public.

In my opinion, Cycle dog food from the Pet Foods Division of General Foods Corporation is a classic example of such behind-the-scenes revelations. Despite the glitter and gold that General Foods and its advertising agencies could bring to the product, well — it just never really paid off.

The story, which appeared in Advertising Age *July 19, 1982, was edited considerably, and, of more concern, a full page of typed text was inadvertently left out in the middle of the story. Here's the full story, as originally written. I think it contains some sobering lessons for marketing management too eager to push a new product into the marketplace.*

Setting the Stage

The Pet Foods Division of General Foods Corporation had an operating profit of $35 million on established brands in fiscal year 1974, I've been told by a former top-level GF executive who was there at the time. In fiscal 1981, the division had an operating loss of $12 million, as estimated by a prominent financial analyst in Chicago. Lots of things, of course, contributed to that dramatic reversal, but the most conspicuous — and probably most important — was Cycle dog food.

This is an insider's story of Cycle's development, marketing strategy, and the going-in miscalculations that haunt GF's marketing management to this day. The moral: Having an enormous amount of money to spend doesn't mean you can buy marketing happiness in the pet food industry," or — from an advertising agency's point of view — "The client can hand you a dandy, built-in copy platform and huge budgets, but that doesn't necessarily mean you can advertise him out of a hole he dug for himself [in Topeka, Kansas]."

Let's start by positioning Cycle canned dog food, which has been in national distribution since spring 1976. (A dry, bagged version was rolled out two years later.) The concept is that a dog's diet should be adjusted according to its position in the life cycle. So, there were four Cycle products: Cycle 1, "specially balanced for puppies up to 18 months of age"; Cycle 2 for adult dogs 1-7 years of age; Cycle 3 for less active (read: overweight) dogs; and Cycle 4 for older dogs (over 7 years).

The original Cycle canned line, which was taken national, had two varieties, beef and chicken; so for the concept to be fully expressed on the shelf, a store had to stock a minimum of eight items. Two facings on each meant 16 items, and so on. And, obviously, if one of the items (or Cycles) was delisted because of slow movement, the whole concept started to unravel. We'll come back to that.

The canned Cycle product is a formed product, common in the dog food packing industry; it's meant to convey the impression of a meatball, such as humans might eat, say, on spaghetti. These balls are packed in a gravy-like sauce, and through time such products have been promoted as "the dog food that doesn't look like dog food."

It should be noted that, historically, other packers who have gone the meatball route have had, at best, lackluster success in the marketplace, and many died aborning. It's a long list, but here are some prominent examples: the original Recipe Balanced Dinners line from Campbell Soup's Champion Valley Division, Rival Tasty Chunk Dinners from Nabisco, the original Skippy Premium line from National Pet Food, and — ironically — Gaines Supreme, a GF brand test marketed before Cycle. Neither Alpo nor Kal Kan, the leading brands in the canned dog food market, carries a meatball item in its extensive line. The reason: slow movement.

And, finally, Cycle canned from the beginning was priced significantly higher than Alpo's Beef Chunks, the leading premium priced canned item, then and now.

The Topeka Plant

One of the main characters in Cycle's passion play is a 150,000 square foot canned dog food plant GF's Post Division started to build in Topeka, Kansas, in November 1971, adjoining a plant GF had built two years earlier on a 110-acre plot to produce dry dog food.

This canned plant, which came on line in May 1973, is a classic example of putting the cart before the horse. At the time the Topeka investment was authorized — circa summer 1971 — GF's Pet Foods

Division did not have a proven canned product for the plant to produce. What it had instead was a product concept in test and, in retrospect, a lot of wishful thinking.

The original hope was a meatball line called Gaines Supreme, which GF put into test market in Buffalo and Albany in March 1970, with Ogilvy & Mather as the agency. For those not familiar with this product class, Gaines is an old and esteemed name in the dog food world. GF has it via the 1943 acquisition of a regional dry packer in Sherburn, New York, and GF still markets a line of dry products under the Gaines name (which, incidentally, will surface again later in our story).

Gaines Supreme didn't do well in Buffalo/Albany, so two years later two new test markets (Miami and Denver) were opened.

No doubt, GF had grandiose plans for Gaines Supreme. At first, they used Arlene Francis as a product spokesperson, but later they reportedly cut a deal with singer/actress Doris Day, "a well known dog fancier," that called for $1 million over five years to tout Gaines Supreme.

There was a hang-up, however: Gaines Supreme died in test market (with less than a 5 percent share of canned pounds), and that left a big capital investment in the prairies of eastern Kansas gathering dust.

Enter Cycle

But, across the plains of Kansas and the White Plains in Westchester County, New York, another concept came barking: Cycle, "every day, for the life of your dog."

The name and concept originated with a small advertising agency, John Rockwell & Associates, which was brought into GF by William E. Rawlings. Mr. Rawlings was president of the Pet Foods Division from 1971 to January 1974, at which time he left after a much publicized wrangle with the president of GF, James L. Ferguson. Mr. Rawlings reportedly was pushing for a faster expansion of GF's pet food business and felt top management was sluggish in approving new moves.

Mr. Rockwell, who had been executive vice president of Needham, Harper & Steers before setting up his own shop, specialized in ginning up new products. He was on retainer to GF from October 1969 to April 1971.

The Cycle concept, according to research, showed that "dog owners are highly anthropomorphic — quick to attribute human traits to their pets — and would respond to a canned line that delivered nutrition specially formulated to the dog's age and 'life style.' " If it succeeded, it would be a good market segmentation and differentiate the Cycle brand from competition — and it was something agency creatives could really get their teeth into. Mr. Rockwell recently told me he envisioned the concept executed in all three product forms — canned, dry, and semi-moist.

(The deliberations GF marketing people were going through in early 1970 trying to decide how best to approach the canned dog food market are documented, apparently factually, in a case study used at the Harvard Business School and The Wharton School, University of Pennsylvania. Included in this 37-page manuscript are the findings of a large-scale GF market segmentation study of dog owners, which sets the framework for execution of the Cycle concept.)

First Test Market

GF took its first version of Cycle canned into test market in Grand Rapids and Sacramento in early 1973, and the product was assigned to Grey Advertising, which was the agency of record until earlier this year when the product (both canned and dry) was moved to Benton & Bowles.

The first test had four Cycle products, but no flavors. "That's what we learned," says Richard O'Brien, who was the Cycle account executive at Grey from the beginning; "you have to give the consumer flavor variety." They also learned that test results projected out to about 4.5 percent share of the canned market, not enough volume to provide a reasonable payout on the brand.

Back to the drawing board. An expanded Cycle line — this time with beef and chicken varieties — was put into a new test area (Syracuse, New York) in April 1974, and later that year it was expanded to a GF sales region that encompassed Boston; Providence, Rhode Island; Hartford, Connecticut; and Portland, Maine. There it sat until April 1976, when the national roll-out started.

I've been told by a GF executive who was deeply involved that between $2 and $3 million was spent on marketing research alone in those test markets. One reason was the length of the test, and another was the low incidence level of target populations — households with puppies, with overweight dogs, etc. Since continuous, diary-type purchase panels were set up to track trial and repeat purchase rates, the screening costs alone were astronomical.

The Magic Number

The "magic number" several GF executives have told me was 6 percent; that was the share of canned pound market that seemed necessary to jell the payout plan on Cycle. I've been told that, in fact, the Syracuse test market did project out to a 6 percent national share. I have also seen data that suggest that in the larger New England region, Cycle only got a 4.7 percent share in the first year. Also, I've been told that the Pet Foods Division's market research department (MRD) felt that test market results were "minimally acceptable," and even after making liberal estimates of the volume to expect, MRD felt that the brand would only achieve in national distribution about 50 percent of the volume the Pet Foods marketing people anticipated. MRD's conclusion: "Don't go national." ("I doubt that," one ex-GF pet food executive told me; "the system would have flagged such a recommendation from MRD, and I didn't know about it.")

Trial in New England seemed good — about 40 percent of the dog-owning households had tried at least one can of Cycle in the first year. And, indeed, much money had been spent to induce trial — about $500,000 annually in spot TV alone in the New England markets. (The same effort now would probably cost over $1 million.)

Was it that MRD was especially conscious of how much Cycle was sold as deal merchandise, and the extraordinary amount of money that was spent to achieve those levels? Or was it, as one GF executive has suggested, a fear of rolling out in a recession economy? In whatever case, going national was what an ex-marketing manager for the Pet Foods Division recently termed "a difficult and somewhat contentious decision."

It all seems to boil down to, "Why, in a high velocity product class like canned dog food, did it take two years of testing to determine if Cycle canned was go or no-go?" It certainly didn't take the Topeka plant that long to pack the required shelf-stocking quantities.

And the really key question is, "If it was a borderline decision, how much was it influenced by that under-utilized plant in Topeka?" — now nearly three years old, which one ex-GFer recently characterized as "that magnificent monument to futility."

"Phil Smith [Philip L. Smith, president of GF's Pet Foods Division at the time] was too hard-headed a guy to let a factory influence such a spending recommendation," says one GF executive who was in on the decision making. But another says flat out, "I doubt Cycle would have been taken national except for that plant."

In any case, the go-national decision was made by GF's Management Committee, which included GF's president at the time, James L. Ferguson.

Heavy Expenditures

The national launch was in April 1976, at the start of a new GF fiscal year. The Maxwell House Division, GF's traditional cash cow, was particularly flush due to a runup in inventory and futures values caused by a severe frost in Brazil, which damaged coffee trees and the yet-to-be-harvested crop. The economy was improving, and it seemed an advantageous time to go out and buy a sizable share of the canned dog food market.

The much-heralded Cycle introduction was estimated at $18 million, with $12 million in advertising and the balance in promotions. It is estimated that 200 million coupons were dropped, and waves of Donnelley's Carol Wright co-op were used, with some coupons having values as high as "one free with one." The cost of goods, laydown, and redemption on such an effort is awesome, especially in the context of the canned dog food business, 1976.

Alpo, which had been the most heavily advertised canned dog food, spent $9 million in measured media in 1976. In just nine months (April-December), Cycle spent $13 million, giving it a 26 percent share of voice in the category for the year.

In 1977, the heavy spending continued — $9.7 million in measured media — making it the most heavily advertised canned brand. This translated into a 23 percent share of voice in the category, compared to a share of pound volume of about 5 percent. Put another way, Cycle canned sales at retail were about $43.2 million in 1977. With an ad expenditure of $9.7 million, that gave Cycle an advertising/sales ratio of 22.4 percent. The other leading premium priced canned brands were running at an A/S ratio of from 4 to 7 percent.

I asked a top executive at Grey Advertising if GF had a share of voice goal. "No," he replied, "they pooh-poohed share of voice at GF; we looked at the absolute expenditures needed to achieve goals [i.e., trial and awareness]. We wanted to burn the concept in, whatever the cost." (An ex-marketing manager at GF refutes this: "We did too pay attention to share of voice," he told me recently.)

But it was the Cycle deal levels that were most impressive, especially to established canned dog food packers. Right from the start and on through 1977, month after month, over 35 percent of Cycle canned was sold as consumer recognized deal merchandise, meaning that a coupon, or off-label price, or advertised store special price was influencing the transaction. Now, that may not seem high compared to some other product classes, but in the canned dog food business in 1976/77, the category average was about 16 percent, and would have been lower if Cycle wasn't included.

GF's direct sales force did a good job; Cycle was quickly pushed into national distribution. (In fact, the Pet Foods Division was an outgrowth of the Post Division at GF, and it was Post's sales force that took Cycle out.)

Signs of Weakness

This spending/selling binge really did a job. In one 28-day period in the summer of 1976, 2.9 million dog owning households bought at least one can of Cycle (which translates into 25 percent of all households that bought any canned product at all). In contrast, 2.3 million households bought some Alpo, the best selling brand. That pace tapered off, and towards the end of 1976, about 1.5 million households were buying some Cycle in a 28-day period. Another thing that Pet Foods management learned about then was that Cycle ingredient costs were running much higher than predicted.

Beneath the surface, a disturbing signal started to flash — at least to those who were watching closely. The average household that purchased Cycle bought about 5 pounds in a 28-day period; the comparable figure for Alpo was 9 pounds, and for Kal Kan, 12 pounds. What this suggested, of course, was that the huge expenditures to induce trial were getting fine penetration for Cycle, but the brand was either reaching relatively light users of canned dog food or people who were not too committed to the brand and/or concept but who were simply reacting to juicy trial offers. (By 1978, the figure had moved up to about 7.5 pounds as the number of households purchasing dropped down to a 1.4 million level every 28 days, but it was still way lower than Alpo or Kal Kan.) Also, it turned out that Cycle had a better penetration of households owning one dog than it did of households owning two or more dogs.

In any case, Cycle share of the total canned pound market progressed as follows: 4.9 percent in 1977; 5.4 percent in 1978; 6.1 percent in 1979; 5.9 percent in 1980; and 6.5 percent in 1981.

Advertising pressure on Cycle canned dropped off to $6.1 million in 1978 and $6.9 in 1979, but the A/S ratio was still at 12 percent, way above the category average of about 3 percent.

Cycle Dry

Buoyed by what on the surface appeared to be a successful launch of Cycle canned, the Pet Foods Division put a Cycle dry version into test market in Syracuse in April 1976 (again, at the start of a GF fiscal year). Since Cycle canned also had been tested in Syracuse, this enabled Pet Foods MRD to measure the cross-purchasing between the canned and dry products.

The dry Cycle was rolled into national distribution in the spring of 1978, and GF was talking about a total budget of $34 million to support the line.

Going into dry form presented a concern. Most nationally promoted, premium priced, dry dog food brands are packed in four sizes: 5, 10, 25, and 50 pounds. Now, if the Cycle concept was fully expressed in the dry dog food section of a supermarket, that would mean stocking at least 16 items just to get one shelf facing on each. This would have been a very tough sell, indeed. (I should add, many supermarkets — especially in the East — do not stock 50-pound bags.)

GF backed off; in the beginning Cycle dry was available in just two pack sizes, 5 and 25 pounds. While this curtailed the brand's reach, at least it left the sales force with something other than an impossible mission. (Later, Cycle dry was made available in a 10-pound pack in western markets.)

In any case, the introduction of a dry line highlighted one of the problems with the Cycle concept: You had to get and hold shelf space on a lot of items to make it fully effective. This is no problem if the brand and individual items have a sizable share or fast turnover. But, with a low share and a sluggish turnover, individual items are always running the risk of being delisted, and — poof! — there goes the concept.

I asked an ex-GF executive if there had been any worry about this in Pet Foods marketing. "Yes," he said, "we talked about it, but we thought we could overcome the problem." Was the GF sales force consulted, I wondered? "Not until we were well down the road," was the answer; "marketing made those decisions." Another executive added, "It was rare that marketing consulted sales, but the shelf-space problem was well recognized."

All of this is of special concern because during the general time period Cycle dry was going national, all hell was breaking loose in the dry dog food market. Ralston Purina was introducing Fit 'n Trim, Kal Kan was taking out Mealtime, Allen Products was introducing Alpo Beef Flavored Dinners, and Quaker was introducing its innovative new product, Tender Chunks, with a campaign estimated at $29 million. In a word, the fight for new listings and shelf space was intense, and in that context the GF sales force had to get more shelf space than their product's sales might justify. Tough.

Great credit to that sales force, however; they did a good job. But I doubt the Cycle concept had as much charm for them as it did to marketing management back at The Plains, or to Mr. Rockwell.

Anyway, as Cycle dry continued to build share of market in the summer/fall of 1978, the amount of goods moving as consumer recognized deal merchandise was extremely high: about 50+ percent, as compared to a category average of about 26 percent. By the late fall, 1.7 million households were buying at least one package of Cycle dry in a 28-day period (about 13 percent of all dry buyers), but as with Cycle canned, they did not buy nearly as much Cycle pounds per period as, say, a Purina Chow buyer would buy of Chow. Again, the data suggested that Cycle was not, relatively, getting to the heavy user.

Changes in 1981

All sorts of doctoring was done on Cycle canned in 1981. The can was downsized. A new flavor, liver, was added to the line. The label was redesigned — for the fourth time in five years — and a little Gaines logo was added, as if that might make a difference. Originally, Cycle was labeled "chunk." This was changed to "dinner of beefy chunks and beef gravy." To use the word "dinner" on a dog food label, a product must have 25 percent or more meat content. Later label designs dropped "dinner" and went to "flavor," which can be used with less than 25 percent meat.

Also, at this stage of its development, it was becoming more and more difficult to find grocery buyers who paid list price for Cycle canned (or dry). The trade deals were so staggered a retail chain could buy discounted merchandise almost continuously.

In early 1982, there was considerably more change. Ralph L. Cobb, a group vice president at GF, was brought in as president of the Pet Foods Division, replacing Robert Sansone. The Cycle account was switched from Grey Advertising to Benton & Bowles as part of a "consolidation," but that didn't seem to matter much since the advertising budget for Cycle had been cut back to nearly nothing. The marketing staff in the Pet Foods Division was drastically reduced, down to about one-fourth its previous size.

Cycle 2 Revisited

To confound matters, GF started to launch in January of 1982 a new canned "meatball" line called Gravy Train, which has "all the appeal of a homemade meal." The GF promotional literature says the initial six months' advertising and promotional package will be $17 million.

If you look closely at the ingredient statement and the guaranteed analysis on the new Gravy Train beef-flavor item and compare it with the same on Cycle 2 ("specially balanced for adult dogs 1-7 years") beef flavor, you'll see that they are, for all practical purposes, identical. Cut the cans and you'll see they look alike.

Full Circle

If you'd like to know who was responsible for the Cycle situation at GF, it's interesting to note that since 1971, when the Pet Foods Division was set up separate from the Post Division, there have been five presidents: William E. Rawlings, Philip L. Smith, Edward Fuhrman, Robert Sansone, and, as of February 1982, Ralph L. Cobb. (Mr. Cobb, ironically, was president of the Post Division — of which pet foods was part — in the late 1960s when John Rockwell sold the Cycle concept to GF.)

Two of those division presidents (Rawlings and Fuhrman) are no longer with General Foods. David Hurwitt, who was marketing manager of the Pet Foods Division when Cycle canned went national, is now in France with GF International. Irving M. Saslaw, who was marketing and development manager for pet foods at the time and who was most directly involved in managing the development of the Cycle product, is now with GF's Technical Center in Tarrytown, New York, as group director/strategic technical planning. Mr. Smith, who was division president when Cycle went national, is now president and chief operating officer at GF; James L. Ferguson, president of GF through the Cycle era, is now chairman and chief executive officer. And Mr. Rockwell, Cycle's inventor, is with Booz Allen & Hamilton, the consulting firm, in New York.

I spoke with Mr. Cobb immediately after an annual meeting of Pet Foods Division executives in Chicago the week of June 21, 1982, and he emphasized that, "We still have confidence in the Cycle concept; it has lots of vitality that we have not obtained." He says that Pet Foods marketing management is in the process of "re-staging" the Cycle business, and, towards that end, a new piece of advertising copy is now being market tested. "We might start advertising again by the end of this year," he adds.

Go into almost any supermarket in the U.S. today, and you'll probably find numerous shelf facings of Cycle product, well positioned. But, if you dig beneath that superficial appearance of success, you'll find an inherently weak brand that got off on the wrong foot 12 years ago and survives today more from marketing push than consumer pull. Over that time, GF's Pet Foods Division has had an extraordinarily large marketing staff, huge marketing budgets by industry standards, an apparently single-minded obsession with a formed "meatball" type product, and an extraordinarily high turnover in top management.

Somewhere, somehow, there must be someone in the upper echelons of GF corporate management who looks down and thinks maybe, just maybe, canned dog food should be lumped into the same category with Viviane Woodward, Kohner Bros., Burger Chef Systems, and W. Atlee Burpee Company — other ill-fated GF expansion efforts of the late 1960s.

Chapter 5

President Reagan's Marketing Plan

I first became interested in the use of survey research — what media often call "political polling" — and its application in developing the marketing plan for aspirants to high political office during the Nixon campaign of 1968.

Since then, every four years, it has become increasingly evident that the "marketing" of political personalities has come to be every bit as well financed and sophisticated as the marketing of non-human goods and services; maybe more so, in some cases. This development reached a new high during the presidential campaign of Ronald Reagan in 1979; no other consumer research program in the political sector has come close to being so well funded or sophisticated.

I had been in touch with his advisors in this area at the time, one being Vincent J. Breglio, executive vice president of Decision / Making / Information, the California-based survey research firm that masterminded the program, from the Republican nominating convention on. But, immediately after the election, when I asked Mr. Breglio for more details, I was overwhelmed by his offer: I could come to their headquarters in Washington, D.C., and review the now famous Black Book (a campaign marketing plan written by Richard B. Wirthlin, president of DMI, and deputy campaign director for strategy and planning in the Committee to Elect), and then review all the survey data that had been done, state by state, in the closing phases of the campaign. This was unprecedented; never before had the planners of a presidential campaign made such a detailed revelation to any publication exclusively. In effect, Advertising Age *had come into possession of instant history, in awesome detail, of what was going on behind the scenes and the information candidate Reagan and his political advisors had at their disposal at various stages of the campaign.*

Rance Crain, editor of Advertising Age, *was quick to recognize the significance of this, and the* Advertising Age *issue of December 15, 1980, carried in its main news pages one of the longest stories in the history of the publication; it ran four full pages, with tables and charts.*

As a by-product of all this, Richard B. Wirthlin was named by the editors of Advertising Age *as Advertising Man of the Year for 1980, a tribute to his key role in planning Ronald Reagan's stunning success. Mr. Wirthlin is the only researcher who has been so honored.*

The Development of Reagan's Marketing Plan

Having full access to internal memoranda and the now renowned campaign strategy Black Book makes it possible to look back over history's shoulder and see how campaign problems and challenges were perceived by Gov. Reagan's planners seven months before the general election.

A confidential memo authored by Richard B. Wirthlin, who was to become the campaign's deputy director for strategy and planning, stated on March 28, 1980: "With over a third of the 998 delegate votes needed to nominate now locked into the Governor's column, and with his best primary states now starting to come up on the primary calendar, the general election campaign, from our point of view, starts today. . . ."

The basic points Mr. Wirthlin made in that memo could be considered a preamble to the strategy Black Book, which he wrote two months later:

- Never before has the electorate been as volatile in switching support from one candidate to another; the loyalty of voters runs thin indeed.

- The primaries [to date] have clearly revealed Carter's basic vulnerability.

- In the process of walking through and beyond the hot coals of the Iowa setback, we learned once again that our most effective asset is providing the electorate with in-depth exposure to Ronald Reagan.

- Care must be exercised so that the Governor's criticism of Carter does not come off as too shrill or too personal. We *can* hammer the President too hard, which will spawn backlash.

- While ideology does not cut strongly in the primary contests, it will be a major vote determinant in November. We have no opportunity to win the general election unless we pull substantial numbers of moderate ticket splitters into our column.

Confidential surveys conducted by Wirthlin through his company, Decision/Making/Information (DMI), showed the Reagan base position with various segments of the electorate as of May 1979 as shown in Table 5-1.

Additional benchmark information came from a psychographic study conducted in June 1979 for the Reagan for President Committee. Entitled "A Survey of Voter Values and Attitudes," this study was based on extensive, in-depth personal interviews with 220 registered voters in 20 large cities. The purpose: "to seek to explain some of the motives underlying people's attitudes and opinions. Psychographic variables reflect psychological traits and personal stands, and they reflect a person's general outlook on life." The project director on this study was Vincent J. Breglio, Mr. Wirthlin's partner and executive vice president of DMI.

One of the study's main conclusions: "Reagan voters obtain high scores on the following scales: respect for authority, individualism, and authoritarianism — and a low score on egalitarianism." The study then pointed out that Democrats over age 55 tend to follow the same pattern and, hence, were a prime target for conversion.

This point was later refined to Eastern European ethnic groups living in large cities and explains why — especially at the start of the campaign — Gov. Reagan made highly visible visits to such neighborhoods. "He was not comfortable doing it, but he did it," recalls Mr. Breglio. Later Gov. Reagan decided to stop the practice because "he considered it exploitative of people."

Out of the psychographic study, three groups of special interest to the campaign were identified:

1. Democrats, head of household employed, 35 years and older, earning less than $15,000.

2. Voters who switch towards Kennedy. [The reasoning was that people who vacillated between Carter and Kennedy must not have strong ideological underpinnings since the two men are so disparate.]

Table 5-1   Voter Types, as Predictor of Reagan-Carter Vote

% of Electorate*	Voter Type	% Reagan	% Carter	% Undecided
22	Conservative Republican	85	12	4
7	Moderate/liberal Republicans	69	25	6
13	Conservative ticket splitters	50	41	9
17	Moderate ticket splitters	50	40	10
14	Conservative Democrats	37	58	5
22	Liberal Democrats	25	68	7
6	Hispanics	17	78	5

* Note: Adds to more than 100% because of rounding.

3. Voters who prefer Reagan over both Carter and Kennedy.

Logistically, the lay of the land — as it appeared to Reagan's planners in the spring of 1980 — was that basically states west of the Missouri River were in the Governor's bag, and there was a good chance of carrying Iowa, Texas, and Florida, too. That suggested, then, a concentration of campaign efforts (and public opinion research measures) in the nine big-electoral vote states that could swing the election. These were Illinois, Ohio, Pennsylvania, Texas, Michigan, California, New Jersey, Florida, and New York.

New York was considered a special case; the cost of turning the state around was considered exorbitant, and there were three big "ifs" — (1) if the upstate Republican organization did an outstanding job of turning out the vote, (2) if Rep. John Anderson's position did not fall below 13 percent, and (3) if the very important Jewish vote was more fractured than normal. Consequently, after the early campaign period, the Reagan forces stopped doing their own opinion tracking studies in New York and relied on studies from other sources to stay in touch. As things worked out, Reagan carried the state.

Another key memorandum addressed to Reagan, William J. Casey, and Edwin Meese III was written by Mr. Wirthlin on May 26. Entitled "Strategy for the Doldrums," it advised on the short-term strategy for the six-week period between the end of the primaries and the start of the Republican National Convention. The basic tone was cautious — "Stay away from unnecessary predictions, specifics, and arguable statements."

The Black Book

Pivotal in campaign planning was a 176-page strategy statement authored by Richard Wirthlin and his associates, Vincent J. Breglio and Richard S. Beal, a consultant to DMI. "This was the campaign Bible," notes Mr. Breglio, "and about one-half was based on surveys Richard [Wirthlin] had done for Gov. Reagan before and during the primaries [research expenditures in the primaries were about $400,000], about one-fourth was based on historical voting behavior data, and the balance on practical judgment."

As to public opinion surveys during the campaign, a budget of $1,400,000 was earmarked for four major national studies and continuous tracking studies in nine pivotal states. Part of the statewide survey field work would be handled through DMI directly, and the balance would be via piggy-backing on state-level studies being done for local candidates by another major Republican political survey firm, Market Opinion Research (MOR) in Detroit.

The Black Book, which was finished in June, starts off with 19 "Conditions of Victory," a listing of important "ifs" upon which success would depend. Here are some of the more noteworthy:

- The conservative Republican Reagan base can be expanded to include a sufficient number of moderates, Independents, soft Republicans, and soft Democrats to offset Carter's natural Democratic base and his incumbency advantage.

- The impact of John Anderson on the race stabilizes, and he ends up cutting more into Carter's electoral vote base than into Reagan's.

- The campaign projects the image of Gov. Reagan as embodying the values that a majority of Americans currently think are important in their President — namely, strength, maturity, decisiveness, resolve, determination, compassion, trustworthiness, and steadiness.

- The candidate and/or campaign avoid fatal, self-inflicted blunders.

- The attack strategy against President Carter reinforces his perceived weaknesses as an ineffective and error-prone leader, incapable of implementing policies and not respected by our allies or enemies.

- Inoculate the voters against Carter's personal attacks by pointing out in the early stages of the campaign through surrogates that Carter has in the past, and will in the future, practice piranha politics.

- We can neutralize Carter's "October Surprise." [Because of the 7 a.m. press conference Carter called on the morning of the Wisconsin primary to hint at a hostage solution, the Reagan planners fully believed another such caper would be forthcoming towards the end of the national campaign.]

- The Governor does not personally answer the Carter attacks; that will be the job of the vice presidential candidate and other surrogates.

- He can win the easiest and least expensive minimum of 270 electoral votes with victories in: California, Illinois, Texas, Ohio, Pennsylvania, Indiana, Virginia, Tennessee, Florida, Maryland, Idaho, South Dakota, Wyoming, Vermont, Utah, Nebraska, North Dakota, New Hampshire, Kansas, Montana, New Mexico, Nevada, Arizona, Oregon, Alaska, Iowa, Colorado, Washington, and Maine (320 electoral votes).

At this stage, the Reagan planners were looking forward to a tough, close race and were well aware that, historically, whenever an elected incumbent was challenged in a re-election bid, two-thirds of the time the challenger lost. "Thus," concluded the Black Book, "unseating Jimmy Carter will be extremely difficult, even unlikely."

There followed a recap of some prevailing political wisdom upon which the planners reckoned, to wit: "Older voters are almost twice as likely to vote as are the younger. . . the highly educated are two to three times as likely to turn out as the poorly educated. . . the numerous groups of 'Born Again' Protestants and 'high church' Protestants are very likely to vote, and vote Republican. . . voters in the Mountain, Pacific, Farm Belt, and Great Lakes regions constitute almost one-half the population, and also have the highest turnout probability."

As to target groups — the prime source of Democratic shifters — "The campaign must convert into Reagan votes the disappointment felt by:

- Southern white Protestants

- Blue collar workers in industrial states

- Urban ethnics

- Rural voters, especially in upstate New York, Ohio, and Pennsylvania.

To this portion of the brief, Mr. Wirthlin added this philosophism: "There is a tendency in our increasingly complex and highly technological society to forget that American Democracy is less a form of government than a romantic preference for a particular value structure." Indeed, although the Black Book didn't belabor the point, the election of Carter in 1976 was dramatic evidence of that point of view.

The Issues

A large national survey conducted by DMI in early June cataloged the issues that would probably most influence the American electorate. For instance, Table 5-2 shows the main issues as of June 1980.

Special attention was paid to the so-called "single issue voter," that segment of the electorate that was so predisposed to just one issue that it might determine voting behavior despite political affiliation and the candidate's position on other issues.

As of June 1980, 28 percent of the electorate were broadly categorized as "single issue" voters. Table 5-3 shows the reigning issues among this group.

With a tighter definition of "single issue" voters, people who would be activists, write letters, give money, etc., it was estimated at

Table 5-2 Main Issues Influencing the Electorate as of June 1980

	% Electorate "Very Interested"
Reduce Government spending	75
National defense	72
Federal income tax policy	62
Draft registration	56
Abortion	48
Women's rights movement	33
Ownership of Panama Canal	31

about 10 percent of the electorate, with ERA, gun control, and abortion the prime issues.

Another way to view issue voting was to ask, as was done in the DMI June study, the electorate's perception of the "most pressing national problems." Table 5-4 shows the results.

Out of all this, obviously, reduction of government influence dominated the issue list, no matter how the subject was approached, with national defense running a close second. And these were, of course, the themes Gov. Reagan hammered on endlessly through the campaign.

In terms of awareness, as of June 1980, DMI showed that about 90 percent of the electorate were familiar with the Reagan name; however, about 40 percent felt they knew very little about what he stood for politically. Clearly, there was a mass education job necessary, especially east of the Mississippi.

The most important thing — "the key to the election" in the opinion of Mr. Breglio — was the June study findings in relation to voter expectations. When asked to name "something good" that would happen if Gov. Reagan were elected, 67 percent of those interviewed could state something positive, from their personal point of

Table 5-3 Percentage Breakdown of "Single Issue" Voters on Key Issues as of June 1980

National defense	27%
Reduce Government spending	25
Draft registration	11
Abortion	11
Federal income tax policy	10
Women's rights	7
Ownership of Panama Canal	1
Other	8
	100%

Table 5-4

Most Pressing National Problem(s)	(%)
Improve the economy — general	22
Cut inflation	20
Reduce unemployment/poverty	17
Reduce Government spending	11
Improve Government leadership	11
Improve immigration policy	10
Secure release of hostages	10
Improve general social conditions	9
Solve energy crisis	8
Reduce welfare	8
Reduce taxes	8
Improve national defense	6

* Total exceeds 100% because of multiple answers.

view. In the case of Carter, only 55 percent could name "something good." In other words, about one-half of the electorate could not imagine even one good thing resulting from the re-election of Carter.

On the negative side, when voters were asked to name "something bad" that would happen if Gov. Reagan were elected, 72 percent named something. For Carter's re-election, it was 83 percent. "This was very encouraging at the time," recalls Mr. Breglio, "because it indicated that if people voted their expectations of the future, we would win."

"The only chance Carter had to win," in the opinion of Mr. Breglio, "was to change the electorate's perceptions of the future, to provide a positive vision. When he chose to make Gov. Reagan the main issue, he was lost."

The same questions were asked in three DMI national studies done after the Black Book was written. Table 5-5 shows how the data from all four studies together look.

In the end, Gov. Reagan had a significant lead over Carter in both the larger number of voters who perceived at least something good coming from his election and the smaller number who perceived something bad.

Reagan Approves

Immediately after the Republican National Convention in Detroit, there was a meeting of key Reagan advisors to read and approve the Black Book strategies. "They went through it page by page," recalls Mr. Breglio, "with Gov. Reagan attending."

At this point, the structure of the Reagan-Bush organization was firm, too, with deputy directors as follows: William Timmons,

Table 5-5

	Something "Good" % Naming	Something "Bad" % Naming
If Reagan elected		
June, 1980	67	72
July, 1980	70	85
August, 1980	66	64
September, 1980	66	67
If Carter re-elected		
June, 1980	55	83
July, 1980	39	85
August, 1980	52	77
September 1980	50	78

organization; Richard Wirthlin, strategy and planning; Edwin Meese, policy and issue research; Peter H. Dailey, advertising/media; and Vernon Orr, comptroller. These deputies reported to campaign director William J. Casey. (Later, Stuart Spencer, a political consultant from California who had handled Reagan's gubernatorial campaigns, joined this group.) "The Black Book pertained to strategy only," Mr. Wirthlin told me recently, "and it was up to the deputy directors to devise tactics; if the Black Book had tried to dictate tactics, the campaign would have failed."

Having a plan is one thing, but adhering to it is another, as any marketing manager knows. For instance, "The activists were putting tremendous pressure on Pete Dailey to make and run negative commercials. They wanted to crucify Carter one finger nail at a time," says Mr. Breglio. But the plan called for not attacking Carter's record until after establishing Reagan's credibility as presidential timber, even though Gov. Reagan was "champing at the bit" to go on the offensive. The Reagan-Bush Committee didn't start to air negative TV commercials until October 10.

"The Black Book plan helped Pete Dailey stand his ground," says Mr. Breglio; "there was an accepted rationale for holding off. Timmons, Spencer, Meese, and Wirthlin were particularly adamant about sticking to the plan. And, in the end, it worked."

In the four months between the Republican Convention and November 4, the Reagan-Bush Committee alone spent $29,400,000 on the campaign effort, and there were additional expenditures by the Republican National Committee, which aided the Reagan cause. Annualized, then, this effort would equal a marketing budget of over $100 million. It was spent by a group of men who were basically strangers at the start. They had to learn to work together in a hurry, under pressure, and to manage a part-time staff of over 300. Everyone seems to agree — it was Richard Wirthlin's Black Book plan that held things together.

The Final Predictions

Table 5-6 shows the actual computer output from Decision/Making/Information's simulation model as it was finally run in Santa Ana, California, at 5:09 p.m., West Coast time, on Monday, November 3, 1980. Using "worst case" assumptions, it predicted that Gov. Reagan would have a minimum of 395 electoral votes, Carter a maximum of 140. (The "best case" assumptions run later in the evening predicted a maximum of 480 electoral votes for Reagan.)

"These data were never shown to Gov. Reagan or his advisors because we were too conservative," I was told by Vincent J. Breglio, executive vice president of DMI, the firm masterminding Reagan's research program. "It was too good to be true; we kept checking for errors."

"The first time we used the word 'landslide' out loud was Monday afternoon," recalls Richard S. Beal, a consultant to DMI and director of political information systems for the Reagan-Bush Committee. "We were looking over the latest runs in our hotel room in California, and it was very exciting. Two Spanish-speaking maids came in to clean the room, and we told them it was going to be a runaway election. They couldn't understand, and probably thought we were crazy."

Modeling

A computer base in DMI's Santa Ana office was the home of survey research studies being conducted by Republican candidates in most key states. In some states, there were continuous telephone surveys being conducted by the Reagan-Bush Committee, either through DMI directly, or through Market Opinion Research in Detroit. In some states where the Reagan-Bush Committee did not have its own poll data, those of Republican candidates running in statewide elections were used as available, as well as studies conducted by other third parties, such as local media, etc. (Each source was examined for research standards before its data were admitted to the system.)

Through a voter simulation model, DMI was to manipulate these data, asking the computer to calculate the changing impact of key assumption variables, such as how the undecided vote, or the Anderson vote, might distribute at the last minute, or the effect of an especially light or heavy voter turnout.

In the "worst case" data shown in Table 5-6, for instance, the going-in assumption was that more of the undecided vote and the

Table 5-6   Final Simulation Model 'Worst Case' Predictions

State	EV	Reagan Margin	Reagan EV	Carter EV	Toss Up	Reagan %	Carter %	Anderson %
Large Electoral States								
California	45	9.1	45	0	0	49.6	40.5	9.9
Illinois	26	14.6	71	0	0	53.0	38.4	8.6
Michigan	21	8.8	92	0	0	50.4	41.6	8.0
New York	41	−13.5	92	41	0	40.4	53.9	5.7
Ohio	25	6.6	117	41	0	49.8	43.2	7.0
Pennsylvania	27	6.8	144	41	0	50.3	43.5	6.2
Texas	26	17.1	170	41	0	57.3	40.1	2.6
Medium Electoral States								
Florida	17	8.1	187	41	0	51.8	43.7	4.5
Georgia	12	−23.8	187	53	0	35.4	59.2	5.3
Indiana	13	20.5	200	53	0	58.2	37.7	4.2
Louisiana	10	9.0	210	53	0	53.3	44.3	2.4
Maryland	10	− 2.6	210	63	0	43.8	46.5	9.7
Massachusetts	14	− 0.6	210	77	0	42.3	42.9	14.7
Minnesota	10	− 4.1	210	87	0	42.5	46.6	−10.9
Missouri	12	7.4	222	87	0	51.2	43.8	5.0
New Jersey	17	20.9	239	87	0	55.2	34.3	10.6
North Carolina	13	−12.9	239	100	0	42.0	54.9	3.1
Tennessee	10	− 2.1	239	110	0	47.8	49.9	2.3
Virginia	12	17.7	251	110	0	55.8	38.0	6.2
Wisconsin	11	4.5	262	110	0	49.6	45.0	5.4
Small Electoral States								
Alabama	9	1.8	271	110	0	49.8	47.9	2.3
Alaska	3	30.2	274	110	0	62.8	32.6	4.6
Arizona	6	23.9	280	110	0	59.9	35.9	4.2
Arkansas	6	5.0	286	110	0	51.0	46.0	3.1
Colorado	7	22.3	293	110	0	56.9	34.7	8.4
Connecticut	8	12.6	301	110	0	51.0	38.4	10.6
Delaware	3	− 1.5	301	113	0	43.7	45.2	11.1
Hawaii	4	− 1.8	301	117	0	45.1	46.9	8.0
Idaho	4	45.2	305	117	0	70.1	24.9	5.0
Iowa	8	10.1	313	117	0	51.8	41.6	6.6
Kansas	7	20.7	320	117	0	56.9	36.2	6.9
Kentucky	9	−13.4	320	126	0	42.2	55.6	2.3
Maine	4	− 1.2	320	130	0	42.9	44.1	13.1
Mississippi	7	9.3	327	130	0	54.2	45.0	0.8
Montana	4	15.9	331	130	0	54.2	38.2	7.6
Nebraska	5	21.9	336	130	0	57.3	35.4	7.3
Nevada	3	39.4	339	130	0	65.0	25.6	9.4
New Hampshire	4	27.5	343	130	0	57.8	30.3	12.0
New Mexico	4	9.4	347	130	0	50.2	40.8	9.1
North Dakota	3	25.4	350	130	0	55.1	29.7	15.2
Oklahoma	8	19.8	358	130	0	58.0	38.2	3.9
Oregon	6	5.6	364	130	0	48.3	42.7	9.0
Rhode Island	4	− 9.4	364	134	0	36.4	45.8	17.7
South Carolina	8	7.6	372	134	0	52.1	44.6	3.3
South Dakota	4	18.4	376	134	0	56.2	37.7	6.1
Utah	4	53.9	380	134	0	73.5	19.6	7.0
Vermont	3	0.1	383	134	0	44.1	44.0	11.9
Washington	9	9.8	392	134	0	50.4	40.6	9.0
West Virginia	6	− 9.3	392	140	0	43.2	52.5	4.3
Wyoming	3	32.8	395	140	0	61.9	29.2	8.9

last-minute switches away from Anderson would go to Carter than Reagan. (In fact, a post-election study based on just people who actually voted showed that the last-minute undecided vote went 43 percent Carter, 42 percent Reagan, and 5 percent Anderson.)

13 States to Carter

The "worst case" prediction showed 13 states with 140 electoral votes going to Carter — New York, Georgia, Maryland, Massachusetts, Minnesota, North Carolina, Tennessee, Kentucky, Maine, Rhode Island, Delaware, Hawaii, and West Virginia. (In fact, just six of those states — Georgia, Minnesota, Maryland, West Virginia, Hawaii, and Rhode Island — plus the District of Columbia, for a total of 49 electoral votes, went to Carter.)

The most important of these, New York with its 41 electoral votes, was a special case. The campaign planners had decided that the cost of campaigning in New York was exorbitant, as related to the chances of success, so after the early campaign stages, no money was spent doing continuous telephone tracking studies there. The research data in DMI's model came from other sources, including studies done by public polling operations, such as Gallup and Harris. Also, the decision was made not to spend advertising money in New York except as necessary to reach Connecticut and New Jersey.

To win New York, the planners felt, three things had to happen: (1) the upstate organization had to do an especially good job in turning out the vote; (2) Anderson's share of the popular vote could not drop below 13%; and (3) the Jewish vote had to fracture, not be as monolithic as normal. A post-election study showed that nationwide about 30 percent of the Jewish vote did go for Reagan, the largest share a Republican presidential candidate has ever received. Presumably, something like that happened in New York State, too. Reagan ended up carrying the state.

An 11-Point Spread

For 18 days before the November 4 vote, Decision/Making/Information, the research firm tracking public opinion for the Reagan-Bush Committee, was conducting 500 telephone interviews a day nationally; this was increased to 1,000 a day over the final three days, November 1-3. Both the November 2nd and November 3rd readings predicted Gov. Reagan would have an 11-point spread over Jimmy Carter in the popular vote. (see Figure 5-1)

In fact, Reagan won with 51 percent of the popular vote, compared to Carter's 41 percent — a 10-point spread. Of all national polls for which data are publicly available, the closest was the ABC/Harris Poll, conducted by Louis Harris, which at the last predicted Reagan winning with a 5-point margin.

Figure 5-1 How the Reagan Polling Went: Final Projection
Oct. 17—Nov. 3

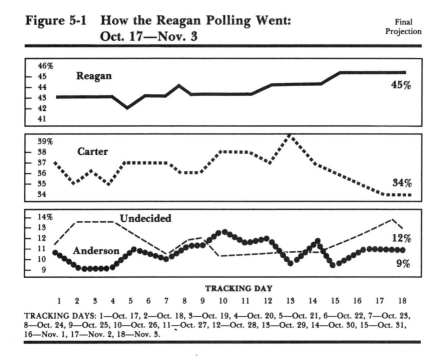

TRACKING DAY

1 2 3 4 5 6 7 8 9 10 11 12 13 14 15 16 17 18

TRACKING DAYS: 1—Oct. 17, 2—Oct. 18, 3—Oct. 19, 4—Oct. 20, 5—Oct. 21, 6—Oct. 22, 7—Oct. 23, 8—Oct. 24, 9—Oct. 25, 10—Oct. 26, 11—Oct. 27, 12—Oct. 28, 13—Oct. 29, 14—Oct. 30, 15—Oct. 31, 16—Nov. 1, 17—Nov. 2, 18—Nov. 3.

More important, in post-election agonizing, public pollsters have tended to claim that their final predictions, which widely missed the mark, were thrown off by a massive, last-minute voter shift to Reagan. The DMI data refute this; they show that Reagan was holding a consistent 5 to 7-point lead over Carter during the period October 17-October 19, and that then started to open up, day by day, to the ultimate 10-point margin.

The undecided vote, shown at about 12 percent of the electorate on election eve, eventually split 43 percent Carter, 42 percent Reagan, and 5 percent Anderson, according to a post-election survey of actual voters. There was a surprise in the Jewish vote; about 30 percent voted for Reagan, the best penetration ever achieved by a Republican presidential candidate. The Black vote gave Reagan about 7-8 percent, which is about normal for Republican candidates.

Post-Election Analysis

Within a five-day period after the November 4 election, Decision/Making/Information, the research firm working for the Reagan-Bush Committee, did a telephone survey of 3,000 people who had actually voted in the election. The results of this study, which became available in early December, make possible a comparison with data gathered from prospective voters in three previous surveys conducted by DMI (1,500 interviews each) in June, September, and mid-October.

These data show how Reagan stood with various segments of the electorate at the beginning, and how these perceptions changed as a result of massive advertising, public appearance, and Carter-Reagan debate exposure. And, finally, they capture the impressions (from the post-election study) of what the electorate's perceptions were as they actually voted.

The data in Table 5-7 show that Reagan's strength with self-avowed Democrats changed little over the five-month span, but there was considerable shift in his favor by both avowed Republicans and registered voters who considered themselves "independent." Among voters of various political ideologies, the most dramatic shifts toward Reagan came from voters labeled "very conservative" and "moderate." The post-election analysis showed that of voters considered "somewhat liberal," 28 percent in fact voted for Reagan, and for "very liberal" the number was 20 percent.

These data also show steadily increasing support for Reagan from union members, starting with 30 percent in June, and ending with 43 percent of that group actually voting for him on November 4. In the area of religious identification, Reagan started off in June with less than 40 percent support from both Catholics and the "born again" Protestants; this had increased to 50 percent of both groups by election time.

Reagan's stand on ERA, which supposedly would cost him dearly with female voters, apparently was not a serious impediment; 48

Table 5-7   Reagan's Position Within Voter Segments

Voter Groups	% Registered Voters			% Actual Voters
	June	Sept.	Oct.	Post-Election
Republican	73	70	77	87
Democrat	21	23	22	25
Independent	38	40	44	53
Very conservative	55	64	61	71
Somewhat conservative	52	48	53	64
Moderate	29	39	38	41
Somewhat liberal	23	24	27	28
Very liberal	21	22	19	20
Union members	30	34	35	43
Born again Protestant	38	44	NA*	50
Catholic	36	42	NA	50
Male	37	42	48	55
Female	35	39	39	48
Deep South	49	49	43	51
Border States	36	42	46	50

* Not asked.

percent of women voters supported him on November 4, according to the DMI post-election survey. These data also show that Reagan started off with strong support (49 percent) with voters in Jimmy Carter's Deep South, and that changed little over the next five months. In the border states — Tennessee, Kentucky, West Virginia, et al., the situation was much different; Reagan started off in that region with only 36 percent support, but that increasd to 50 percent by election time.

Throughout the interviewing, prospective voters were asked their impressions of Reagan, Carter, and John Anderson on a battery of traits relevant to a position of presidential leadership. Table 5-8 shows the data, from all four national studies, on how the public perceptions of Reagan were changing over a five-month period.

Most notable is registered voter perception of Reagan as a "strong leader," which had stayed in the 42 percent range prior to the election; however, of people who voted, 61 percent attributed this quality to Reagan at voting time. Another dramatic shift came on the "reduce inflation" issue — with about half the voters giving him that credit prior to the election and 71 percent at election time. The specter of Reagan as a potential warmonger apparently remained constant — 41 percent of registered voters in September thought he "would be likely to start an unnecessary war" and then again in October. In the voting booth, it dropped to 39 percent of actual voters.

The Undecided Vote

Of special interest in the post-election survey of actual voters was the size of the last-minute undecided vote and how that vote distributed among Reagan, Carter, and Anderson. Since DMI had conducted similar surveys after the presidential elections of 1976 and 1972, it was possible to make that further comparison.

As the data in Figure 5-2 show, 46 percent of people who actually voted had decided for whom they would vote nine weeks before Labor Day, which fell on September 1 in 1980. At the time of the

Table 5-8 Voter Perception of Reagan on Leadership Traits

Perceived Traits	% Registered Voters			% Actual Voters
	June	Aug.	Oct.	Post-Election
Strong leader	42	45	42	61
Trustworthy	NA	29	39	33
Reduce inflation	46	53	NA	71
Would be likely to start unnecessary war	NA	41	41	39
Cares about elderly/poor	27	26	—	26

Figure 5-2

When Did the Electorate Make Up Its Mind to Vote for Presidential Candidates:
1972 - 1976 - 1980 Compared

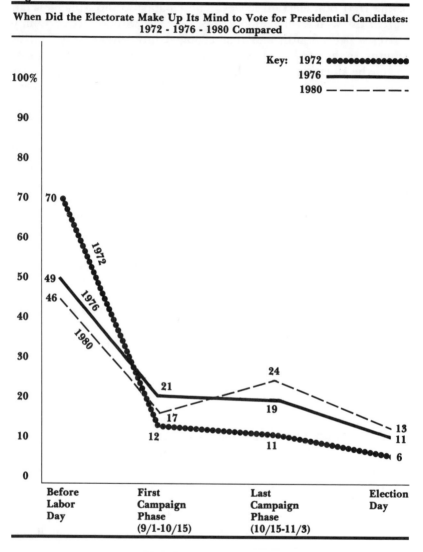

election on November 4, 13 percent were still undecided (as compared to 11 percent in 1976 in the Carter-Ford election).

This 13 percent last-minute undecided vote split 43 percent to Carter, 42 percent to Reagan, and 5 percent to Anderson. The balance (10 percent) was distributed among a variety of splinter party candidates.

These data, of course, go counter to the so-called "big bang" thesis held by Carter's research expert, Patrick Caddell, and others, saying that there was a massive last-minute shift of this vote to

Reagan. Mr. Caddell has been quoted as saying his data showed that eight million voters shifted to Reagan during the last two days of the campaign, a thesis also held by Warren Mitofsky, the director of the polling effort run by CBS News and shared by *The New York Times*.

Chapter 6

The Big Four
of Political Research

Just four men — Richard B. Wirthlin, Robert M. Teeter, Peter D. Hart, and Patrick H. Caddell — dominate political survey research, or "polling," in the U.S. For instance, during the mid-term elections of 1981-82, these four, and the organizations behind them, worked for 50 senatorial, 163 congressional, and 44 gubernatorial aspirants. In total, these campaigns accounted for about $13 million in political survey research.

No surprise, then, that these four have come to be media personalities in their own right; they are constantly being interviewed by TV commentators and news magazines about the mind set of vox populi *in the United States.*

Yet, to marketers away from the political arena, these four men are relatively unknown. Hence, this article from Advertising Age *of February 28, 1983. Among other things, it included an historic photograph — the first time these four men had been photographed together. Quite appropriately, the photo was taken on a cool, windy day on the west lawn of the White House, where all four wish they had a client in residence — and Richard Wirthlin does.*

The Background of Political Polling

Before, during and after the 1982 elections they seemed omnipresent. *Time, U.S. News & World Report, The New York Times* — and especially *The Washington Post* — quoted them at length. The TV public affairs talk shows sought them as guests, and NBC's "Today" show and ABC's "Good Morning America" brought them into your breakfast nook. They were queried as political gurus and asked to explain *vox populi,* and reporters listened carefully. After all, if these guys couldn't explain the American voter's psyche, hopes and frustrations, who the hell could?

"These guys" are an increasingly prominent genus of survey researchers, or "political pollsters," as the media label them. There

The "big four" of political research (l. to r.): Peter Hart, Patrick Caddell, Richard Wirthlin, and Robert Teeter.

aren't many — maybe a dozen or so operating in the political big leagues. But some — especially Richard B. Wirthlin and Robert M. Teeter on the Republican side of the aisle, and Peter D. Hart and Patrick H. Caddell on the Democratic side — have become media personalities. At first, this was basically fame rub-off from their clients: the congressional, senatorial, gubernatorial, and, above all, presidential candidates. But now, these four have come to have, it seems, a public presence that transcends their association with one or more prominent politicians or the vicissitudes of a specific election wave.

A recent example: Right after President Reagan's State of the Union address to Congress on January 25, Tom Brokaw and Roger Mudd of NBC TV News interviewed a panel of political pollsters — Wirthlin, Hart, and Teeter — on their personal reaction to the political impact of the President's message.

One reason, I suggest, is that more editors and TV producers now realize that as the cost and sophistication of politicking in the United States escalates, these pollsters have huge survey budgets at their disposal to study American society, the undercurrents, the attitudes, and the predispositions that drive economic trends over and beyond immediate election results.

For instance, just the Big Four — Wirthlin, Teeter, Hart, and Caddell — collectively, in the 1981-82 election campaigns (including primaries) fielded public opinion surveys for 50 senatorial, 163 congressional, and 44 gubernatorial aspirants. These candidates spent about $13 million on research, and this is estimated to be 60 to 65 percent of the total spent by all major political candidates.

One extraordinary case in point was the unsuccessful gubernatorial campaign of Lewis E. Lehrman (R) in New York State in 1982 which, according to him, cost $14 million. In excess of $300,000 of that was spent on survey research through Mr. Wirthlin's firm, Decision/Making/Information. Obviously, after such an exercise, the researcher involved becomes extraordinarily knowledgeable about the public mood in New York State — region by region, ethnic group by ethnic group.

So, the likes of Wirthlin, Teeter, Hart, and Caddell have probably become the best financed social scientists in the United States or, perhaps more accurately, the best informed marketers in the sense of relating effective appeals to target market segments.

Marketing Orientation

"Winning elections today is a science, not an art form, and I believe that 10 percent of any campaign budget should be spent up front on public opinion studies — to make sure the other 90 percent is not wasted," opines Richard Richards, past chairman of the Republic National Committee. Mr. Teeter estimates that, on average, it ran about 5 percent in the campaigns he was involved with in '82.

Square that with *Time* magazine estimates that, in 1981-82, U.S. Senate and House candidates alone spent roughly $300 million on their campaign efforts, and that was an increase of about 25 percent over 1980. *Time* went on to say, "When races for governor and state legislative posts are added in, the grand total may hit half a billion dollars."

Hugh Sidey, one of the most respected observers of the presidency, added this prediction in one of his recent *Time* essays: "The upcoming [1984] presidential race will be the longest, most televised, most computerized, most numbing electoral spectacle in history. It could also be the most expensive, exceeding the record $275 million spent in 1980, if Ronald Reagan does not run and the Republican field crowds up with free-spending long shots."

That 1984 race has already started; as of January 1, 1983, stated candidates for the presidency became eligible for federal matching funds. Political operatives are already in place in Iowa, where the first caucuses are tentatively scheduled for February 27, 1984.

Ted Kennedy has bowed out. Walter F. Mondale, Alan Cranston, John Glenn, Gary Hart, and Reubin Askew have announced officially. And, believe it, the campaign managers who "handle" these candidates have basically the same mentality as high-powered marketers of detergents, cigarettes, or beer. Their "product" is a personality who represents a point of view. As for the political pollsters who support these campaigns with data, and in some cases, intimate counsel, they may well spend between $25 and $30 million on political surveys, modeling, and analysis of past voting behavior on behalf of their clients, state committees, and political action groups between now and the '84 election.

The Big Four

As things steam up with the first primary (New Hampshire on March 6, 1984), there will be the Big Four — Wirthlin, Teeter, Hart, and Caddell — pontificating on the ebbs and flows of public opinion. In preparation for that, you may want to learn more about these men — and where they're coming from, as the teenagers say.

Robert M. Teeter

Robert M. Teeter, who turned 44 in 1983, has been in the political arena since the mid-1960s when, as a young instructor in political science at Albion College in Michigan, he put in two summers of volunteer work for George W. Romney, the ex-president of American Motors who became Republican Governor of Michigan.

In 1966, Mr. Teeter joined the Detroit-based survey research firm of Market Opinion Research and devoted most of his time to Gov. Romney's unsuccessful bid for the presidential nomination. This work led to the staffing of a Political Division of MOR which, in 1972, hit the jackpot — management of the survey research program for a President of the United States, Richard Nixon, who was running for re-election. (In the '68 election, Nixon's work was done primarily by Thomas W. Benham at Opinion Research Corporation, Princeton, N.J. In 1972, ORC and Decision/Making/Information did some of the Nixon work.)

"Most of our presentations were made to Bob Haldeman or John Mitchell at the Committee to Re-Elect," says Mr. Teeter, "but some of the meetings were with Nixon personally." For political pollsters, that's the ultimate ego trip — interface with a sitting President.

The election of 1976 found Mr. Teeter and MOR doing all the research for Gerald R. Ford, another sitting President, and by now Mr. Teeter was a familiar face at the Southwest Gate, where most staffers enter the White House.

Concurrently, Mr. Teeter and MOR were building a base in Canadian politics, having done survey research for the Conservative Party in the federal elections of 1972, '74, and '79. And in the United States, MOR has worked for hundreds of Republican political aspirants over the years; in 1982 alone, they were involved in 97 gubernatorial, senatorial, and congressional races.

Today, Mr. Teeter, a stalwart in Republican Party affairs, is most closely associated with Vice President George Bush. "We became friends back in the '70s when he was chairman of the Republican National Committee," says Mr. Teeter, who handled all the survey research for Bush in the presidential primaries of 1980.

Mr. Teeter, who became president of MOR in 1979, lives in Ann Arbor, Mich., with his wife Betsy and their two children. He received his M.A. degree in political science from Michigan State University.

Richard B. Wirthlin

Richard B. Wirthlin, 52, is a soft-spoken, cherubic man with an academic demeanor who currently reigns as the *paterfamilias* of the political research coterie because, bluntly, he has a client — and personal friend — sitting as President of the United States. With that come all sorts of political status symbols, such as flights on Air Force One and data presentations at the Reagan ranch outside Santa Barbara.

Dr. Wirthlin (Ph.D. in economics from the University of California at Berkeley) was chairman of the department of economics at Brigham Young University and director of BYU's Survey Research Center when, in 1968, he first met and did a survey for Ronald Reagan who was serving his first term as Governor of California. The go-between was Richard Richards, at the time head of the Republican Committee in Utah (and upon Reagan's election as President, chairman of the Republican National Committee).

Dr. Wirthlin left academe in 1969 to form a survey research firm, Decision/Making/Information, in Santa Ana, California, along with Paul Newman (now a political consultant in Seattle), Vincent J. Breglio (until recently, executive director, National Republican Senatorial Committee; now president of Research/Strategy/Management, a Washington-based political survey firm), and Vincent Barbarra, who has served twice as director, Bureau of the Census, and now director, marketing intelligence at Eastman Kodak Company.

Through the years, Wirthlin's firm, DMI, has handled the survey research for, literally, dozens of Republican biggies, including Senators Barry Goldwater, Paul Laxalt, Robert Dole, John Tower, and Peter Domenici — and Governors, including the late Nelson Rockefeller.

During Reagan's Presidency, DMI has gotten the lion's share of public opinion survey work that, while paid for by the Republican National Committee, is really designed and destined for political strategists (and the President) within the White House. (Mr. Teeter's firm, MOR, does work for the committee, too.)

This continuous tracking of public opinion is, without doubt, the most extensive ever utilized by an administration. But the scope and detail are played down lest, fear President Reagan's advisors, he appear to be reacting to whims in public opinion instead of imposing his own political leadership. Be that as it may, this part of DMI's work causes Mr. Wirthlin to make the short walk from his personal office in the District over to the White House almost daily to confer with James A. Baker III, Edwin Meese III, Michael K. Deaver, and other presidential advisors.

"Since I've been involved in politics — and that's less than 20 years — there's been a revolution in the way politicians go about running for public office. Some of the changes are good for society, and the country; some concern me," Mr. Wirthlin told me in a recent interview. "On the positive side, I think it's healthy for a democracy when elected officials must listen to their constituencies with an open ear. And political polling is the vehicle that makes it possible. That's healthy."

But, on the negative side, notes Mr. Wirthlin: "I'm concerned about the rising power of television, and how that's weakened the political parties. Also, the cost of running for office has become forbidding. We must find a way to keep the channels to elective office as open as possible."

Because of his work as deputy campaign director of strategy and planning for the Reagan campaign of 1979-80, Mr. Wirthlin was named "Advertising Man of the Year" by *Advertising Age*, the first researcher so honored.

Mr. Wirthlin, his wife Jeralie, and the youngest of their eight children live in McLean, Virginia.

Peter D. Hart

Peter D. Hart, 41, is the only one of the Big Four who hasn't grabbed the White House brass ring — yet. But that could change in 1984. Mr. Hart has done survey work for four Democratic hopefuls — Senators John Glenn, Ernest Hollings, and Alan Cranston, and former Vice President Walter Mondale — and, as he told me recently, "I hope to work for one of them in the next election."

The son of an English professor at the University of California at Berkeley, Mr. Hart came east to attend college (Colby College in Maine; B.A. in history) and stayed to start his political apprenticeship in 1964 as a $75-a-week coder with Louis Harris, the pollster who became famous working for John F. Kennedy in 1960, the first presidential campaign where survey research was an important planning tool.

In 1968, Mr. Hart had his first client: John J. Gilligan in an Ohio Senate race. Then he did off-year surveys for the Democratic National Committee and, in 1970, joined the political polling firm run by the late Oliver Quayle. He returned briefly to Louis Harris and Associates as a vice president before founding his own firm, Peter D. Hart Research Associates, Inc., in the District.

In the years since, Mr. Hart has worked for numerous Democratic politicians, including Edward Kennedy (1980), Henry "Scoop" Jackson, John Stennis, and Illinois Congressman Abner Mikva. In the 1982 elections, Hart's firm worked on 35 senatorial, congressional, and gubernatorial campaigns.

"In recent elections the Republicans have outspent the Democrats about 2½ to 3 to 1 for political polling," says Mr. Hart, "but I don't view that as seriously as some people. It really comes down to understanding the dynamics of a campaign — public perception of the candidate, the key issues, and the qualities voters are looking for in a particular public office. The role of survey research is to understand those dynamics, and in that respect, I don't think the amount of money spent is all that important. I look for 'windows of opportunity' for the candidates we work for, and that may well come from one benchmark survey."

Mr. Hart lives in the District with his wife Florence and their two children.

Patrick H. Caddell

Patrick H. Caddell, 32, the most flamboyant of the Big Four, was named by *Time* magazine in 1974 as one of its 200 "future leaders of the United States," in part for his survey work for George McGovern in his ill-fated campaign of 1972. Now, of course, he is best known as the survey researcher who served President Carter.

Mr. Caddell got started early. As a high school student in Jacksonville, Florida, he worked on an analysis of election returns in the State of Florida as a math project. Notoriety from this work got him an appointment as a special assistant to the speaker of the Florida House of Representatives, while still a high school student.

At age 21 and still an undergraduate at Harvard University, Mr. Caddell — along with some student friends — founded a firm called Cambridge Survey Research, worked in the McGovern campaign, and first met an obscure politician from Georgia by the name of Jimmy Carter. In 1974, he founded a second research firm, Cambridge Reports, to conduct omnibus national surveys for commercial clients.

In 1975, when Carter faced a "showdown" primary battle in Florida against Gov. George Wallace of Alabama, he called on Mr. Caddell, whose knowledge of Florida was well known (his senior thesis at Harvard was on changing trends in southern politics). Carter won, and Mr. Caddell became part of the young, relatively inexperienced team that swept into the White House on Carter's surprise victory. As a young bachelor with a Rolls-Royce and a townhouse in the District's posh Georgetown section, he became well known as a night-life buddy of Jody, Ham, and Stu. (When Hamilton Jordan broke up with his wife, he moved into Mr. Caddell's home.)

Today Mr. Caddell heads his firm, Cambridge Survey Research, and — in addition to political work — is striving to build up a commercial clientele. (He is no longer involved in the other firm, Cambridge Reports.)

In the 1982 elections, he worked for Democratic senatorial, congressional, and gubernatorial aspirants, including Sen. Edward Kennedy's re-election campaign in Massachusetts. Since that front-running prospect for the 1984 presidential race has bowed out, Mr. Caddell makes like the reluctant dragon about '84. "I might do a campaign; it depends on how I feel about the man," he told me recently, but was quick to add, "I did both of Hart's [Sen. Gary Hart of Colorado] campaigns and I've worked for Askew [former Gov. Reubin Askew of Florida]. All of them are friends."

What It All Means

The world of political researchers work in is, in many respects, much different than that of most market or social researchers, and that carries over to the people, too. Here are some observations, for the record.

The political pollsters are very political animals — articulate and skilled at dealing with the press. Generally, they have more of a marketing orientation than many researchers who work in package goods companies. One reason for that is that they are closer to the action, the decision making, and the splattering of blood if something goes wrong. Also, they tend to get more personally involved with their clients and the issues at stake.

Political researchers work horrendously long hours and, especially during the political "season," against very short deadlines. Compared to most market researchers, theirs is a strict winner-takes-all mentality. A marketer, for instance, might launch a new product that has a goal of 5 percent share of market. It might fall short to, say, a 3.5 percent share, but still be worthwhile and profitable. No such grey area exists in political campaigns; only winning counts.

The ultimate ego trip for a political researcher is to latch onto a rising political star and coattail him into the White House — with all that implies with press attention, the attraction of business to his firm, the percs, invitations to speak, and — perhaps — a personal relationship with "the man" that makes the researcher feel that, to some degree, he is a player on the world's stage. But such a win is a long shot, and day to day, a political polling business is built on continuous relationships with state political party committees or national political action (read: funding) groups like the National Republican Senatorial Committee. These groups often select the local slates, advise the candidates, and are in the position to urge the use of (or approve) a particular campaign manager or pollster. This is bread and butter — the over-the-transom work from, literally, hundreds of aspiring Congressmen new to politics who are being coached on how to run a successful campaign.

The increasing clout political survey research plays in this process was summarized by Howell Raines, a political writer for *The New York Times*: "In the new campaign weaponry, polls have become enormously important for novel reasons. For example, to gain entrance to political action committees, which are the 'fat cats' of today's political order, a candidate needs a survey, or at least an encouraging letter, from a big-name polltaker."

Like any good commercial market researcher who cringes when he sees a client ignore or misuse research data — and head over the cliff — a political researcher has the same frustrations. Campaign managers can cut him off from the candidate or read their own personal interpretation into the data. Advertising advisors — often volunteers — can screw up a campaign thrust. And, to a political pollster who has worked on, literally, hundreds of campaigns and seen every mistake and screw-up in the book, it can be very frustrating not to have a dominant voice in campaign operating decisions.

Political researchers tend to be myopic; theirs is a tight, cliquish community. For instance, the impressive sounding National Association of Political Pollsters, which was founded in 1975 to represent the interests of political pollsters with the Federal Election Commission, has just four members — Wirthlin, Teeter, Hart, and Caddell. The by-laws are written in such a way that maybe two other prominent pollsters are qualified to join, assuming they come up with the $2,500 annual fee.

Savvy, a mite world-weary, hard-working, inveterate name droppers — the political researchers drive a growing, prominent segment of the survey research industry. And the press attention has elevated them to research superstar status.

Part II

The U.S. Marketing Research Industry

Foreword

Readers of the marketing case histories in Part I have probably noted that they are peppered with references to marketing, advertising, and public opinion research studies that were providing important inputs to the marketing decisions being made at the time (and, in some cases, being ignored). Moreover, just as much notice was given to the behind-the-scenes research organizations who were involved as was given to the much more prominent, and public, advertising agencies.

Point is: Marketing, advertising, and public opinion research has been inexorably intertwined with the growth of the advertising and, later, marketing industries. To know how the marketing research industry grew and evolved in the U.S. is to know, largely, how the professionalism of marketing grew and evolved; they are really part and parcel of one another. So, a marketing case history — at least in my opinion — just isn't complete unless the marketing research (or lack thereof) behind marketing decisions is known.

Yet, it is just within the past 10 years or so that the size, nomenclature, and diversity of the industry, as it exists in the United States, have come to be commonly known. The reasons are many. For one, until recent years, many of the important firms were privately held, and they did not make their size public. Almost all the work they did was for clients on a proprietary basis and often related to extremely confidential marketing plans or new product development. Another reason was that — and this is still true today — the industry did not have a trade journal of its own that could throw public light on that information about industry happenings that was publishable. And, finally, no one had asked. As is often the case, a lot of the confidentiality was more imagined than real. Put another way, many key people in the industry were, in fact, anxious to have a press that tried to make their good work known and appreciated — within the limits of client restraints and related ethical concerns.

The "press" that developed, largely, was in *Advertising Age*, and that was almost entirely due to the editor-in-chief, Rance Crain, who — starting in the early 1970s — made ample space available for what news was forthcoming from the research industry. In my personal opinion, and of course I'm biased, Mr. Crain was very far-sighted; very little of the material in Part II of this book (or Part I, for that matter) would have seen the light of publishing day but for Mr. Crain's editorial instincts.

But it did grow and become more commonplace as disclosure barriers dropped over the years. The end result is a chronicle of the U.S. research industry, the highlights of which follow.

Chapter 7

The U.S. Research Industry

Gallup, Starch, Nielsen, Roper, Hooper — these names are well known within the marketing community, and even to the general public, to some degree. Unfortunately, little has been written to document how the marketing / advertising research industry got started — way back in the early· 1900s — in the United States, and the roles these now-famous pioneers played.

I tried to briefly summarize the early days in a Research Beat column that appeared in Advertising Age *on April 19, 1976. The story began prior to 1900, and here it is.*

The Early History

Would anybody guess that marketing research goes back nearly to this country's beginnings?

Take political polling. In July, 1824, the *Harrisburg Pennsylvanian* printed a report of a straw vote taken at Wilmington, Del., "without discrimination of parties." In that election year poll, Andrew Jackson received 335 votes; John Quincy Adams, 169; Henry Clay, 19; and William H. Crawford, 9. Later the same year, another newspaper, the *Raleigh Star*, undertook to canvass political meetings held in North Carolina, "at which the sense of the people was taken."

Use of original marketing research by an advertising agency to gain a new account popped up as early as 1879. N. W. Ayer & Son was soliciting the Nichols-Shepard Company, manufacturer of agricultural machinery. Ayer prepared a media schedule that was challenged by the would-be client, according to L. C. Lockley writing in *The Journal of Marketing* for April 1950. Substantiation came from an Ayer survey of state officials and publishers throughout the country asking for information on grain production and media circulation by counties. The client was impressed and Ayer got the account.

In 1895, Harlow Gale of the University of Minnesota was using mailed questionnaires to obtain public opinions on advertising, and George B. Waldron was doing qualitative research for Mahin's Advertising Agency around 1900, according to Mr. Lockley. In 1901, Walter Dill Scott, later president of Northwestern University, undertook a program of experimental research on advertising for the Agate Club of Chicago.

It wasn't until about 1910, according to Mr. Lockley, "that evidences of market research became frequent enough to indicate that a new field of business activity had made a serious start." In 1911, for instance, J. George Frederick left the editorship of *Printer's Ink* to start what may have been the first business research company, the Business Bourse. Among his early clients were General Electric and the Texas Company. By Mr. Frederick's estimates, no more than $50,000 was spent in gathering marketing information, even informally, in 1910.

It was also in 1911 that R. O. Eastman, then advertising manager for the Kellogg Company in Battle Creek, Michigan, interested some members of the Association of National Advertising Managers (as the Association of National Advertisers was then known) to cooperate on a joint postcard questionnaire survey to determine magazine readership. That introduced the important concept of duplication of circulation. Mr. Eastman became so involved in this sort of survey that in 1916 he started his own company, the Eastman Research Bureau. His first clients were *Cosmopolitan* and the *Christian Herald*, followed later by the General Electric Company, which wanted a consumer survey to determine recognition of the "Mazda" trademark.

The year 1911 also saw the establishment of a Bureau of Business Research at the Harvard Graduate School of Business, as well as the now famous Commercial Research Division of the Curtis Publishing Company, headed by Charles C. Parlin. This operation was spun off in 1943 to become the company now known as National Analysts. In 1915, the U.S. Rubber Company started a research department headed by Dr. Paul H. Nystrom, and two years later Swift & Company followed with a department headed by Dr. Louis D. H. Weld.

In the newspaper field, the *Chicago Tribune* pioneered in 1916 with a door-to-door survey of consumer purchasing habits in Chicago. This same paper in the 1950s, under the leadership of Pierre Martineau, sponsored what was probably the largest and most diverse marketing and advertising research staff ever for an advertising medium.

About 1918, the now famous husband-wife team of Percival White and Pauline Arnold started the Market Research Company, which later, under the ownership of Samuel Barton, became known as the Market Research Corporation of America (MRCA).

Some of the more familiar pioneer names in research started to flourish in the 1920s. Dr. Daniel Starch, for instance, first used the recognition method for measuring the readership of advertisements and editorial content in magazines and newspapers in 1922.

Dr. George Gallup also got into advertising readership measurements in 1923, but he is probably best known today for the Gallup Poll, which was first published in 35 newspapers in 1935 and promptly got him denounced as a "charlatan," a fate that also befell such other pioneer pollsters as Elmo Roper and Archibald Crossley.

These men had a common problem: convincing skeptical editors and commercial clients that, indeed, a small sample of the population, if properly drawn, could be used to measure accurately the predilections of society. Led by Dr. Gallup in 1936, they turned to public elections; here was a chance to measure just before a public event where real, tabulated results could be compared with survey predictions. Even with the progress since, sampling methodology today still remains the most baffling mystique associated with marketing research.

A young man by the name of Arthur C. Nielsen entered the marketing research field in 1923. He, in effect, invented the concept of share-of-market, which has held businessmen spellbound ever since; they've spent more to get at that than for anything else in the marketing information field. Result: The A. C. Nielsen Company is today by far the largest marketing research operation in the world.

The 1930s saw an explosion of new companies dedicated to this new thing called "research." Daniel Starch & Staff (now Starch INRA Hooper Inc.) opened its doors in 1932. Also in that period came Lloyd Hall & Associates; C. E. Hooper Inc.; Crossley Inc.; Stewart, Dougall & Associates; Psychological Corp.; Opinion Research Corp.; Willmark Research Corp.; and the American Institute of Public Opinion.

Research was starting to become an American export. Dr. George Gallup set up affiliate relationships with survey companies in England and France in 1936, and A. C. Nielsen started a subsidiary in England in 1939, when World War II started.

War needs spurred the further development of the fledgling research field. Paul Lazarsfeld, the social research scholar, has stressed: "During WW II, social research was in heavy demand by all branches of the government — and especially the Army, the Office of Price Administration, and the Office of War Information (OWI)." Much of the OWI work, Mr. Lazarsfeld noted, was done by contract through the Department of Agriculture, where a young psychologist named Rensis Lickert headed the division of program studies. Social scientists were, more and more, drawn into public opinion and attitude research.

After the war, Mr. Lickert took his team to the University of Michigan to create the now famous Survey Research Center. His counterpart at OWI, research director Elmo Wilson, started his own company, International Research Associates, after the war.

There was a postwar boom in research. Of the Top Ten research companies in the United States in 1976, all but one (Nielsen) were founded after WW II. This period also saw the advent of the electronic computer, which broke open the way to large-scale data manipulation.

This brief history, unfortunately, leaves unmentioned many of the prominent shapers of the research community in the United States today, and many of the landmark texts, events, and contributions that have enriched the field. Nevertheless, it seems evident that marketing and advertising research are more inextricably involved in our country's history than most would guess, except for a backward look prompted by a Bicentennial.

Chapter 8

A. C. Nielsen, Sr.:
Obituary Traces History

In my opinion, no other single man contributed as much to the development of professionalism in marketing as Arthur C. Nielsen, Sr., who died on June 1, 1980, at the age of 82.

In 1923, Mr. Nielsen founded the A. C. Nielsen Company, which today operates through subsidiaries in 24 foreign countries; it's the largest marketing research organization in the world by far. In fact, ACN, in terms of annual revenues, is also much larger than the largest U.S.-owned advertising agency, worldwide.

When I learned that Mr. Nielsen's health was failing back in the spring of 1980, I suggested to Rance Crain, editor of Advertising Age, *that I prepare a suitable obituary to the man so that, when and if the day came, we'd have a substantial tribute ready to publish. Mr. Crain agreed, and I prepared the article that follows — with considerable cooperation from the A. C. Nielsen Company and members of Mr. Nielsen's family.*

Mr. Nielsen's obituary ran in Advertising Age *on June 9, 1980, and despite considerable trimming, it was still the longest such personal tribute ever to run in that publication. Here's the full story of the man who invented the concept of "share of market" — and as you'll see, Mr. Nielsen's professional career is, in large part, a chronicle of the growth of marketing and advertising research around the world.*

A. C. Nielsen, Sr.

WINNETKA, ILL. — *Arthur C. Nielsen, Sr., founder of A. C. Nielsen Company, the world's largest and most renowned marketing/advertising research company, died June 1, 1980. He was 82.*

Mr. Nielsen, who founded the company in 1923, moved from president to chairman in 1957, when he was succeeded by his son, Arthur, Jr. The senior Mr. Nielsen, whose most recent title was chairman of the executive board, had been in ill health for the past few years.

103

Despite the prominence of the Nielsen name — with the general public through the company's broadcast audience ratings service, and with marketing men through its store audit services and coupon clearing house — Mr. Nielsen's extraordinary business and personal achievements have been relatively unheralded, especially over the past 20 years. He was a private man.

In 1923, four years after graduating from the University of Wisconsin with the highest scholastic average (95.8) ever recorded in the college of engineering, and after two years of duty as a naval officer in World War I, Mr. Nielsen started in business with six employees and $45,000 capital raised from a group of friends.

Thus, Mr. Nielsen — at age 26 — became a pioneer in a fledgling industry. Prior to 1923, there were just three U.S. companies specializing in marketing/advertising research: Business Bourse, founded by J. George Frederick in 1911; Eastman Research Bureau, founded by Roy O. Eastman in 1916; and Market Research Company, founded by Percival White in 1918. (Two other research pioneers, Daniel Starch and George Gallup, also started their companies in 1923.)

Today the A. C. Nielsen Co., now public and traded over-the-counter, operates out of its headquarters in Northbrook, Ill., through subsidiaries in 21 foreign countries, and has over 17,000 employees and annual revenues of nearly $400,000,000. In contrast, the world's largest advertising agency, J. Walter Thompson Company, had worldwide revenues of $254,000,000 in 1979. Or, put another way, the Nielsen Company's revenues from marketing/advertising services alone ($286,000,000 in fiscal year 1979) are larger than those of the next seven largest U.S. research companies combined.

More important, Mr. Nielsen's unique blend of foresight, business acumen, inventiveness, and personal bearing has probably done more to shape the professionalism of the worldwide marketing/advertising research industry than that of any other man. He was truly a statesman.

The Dark Days

During its first 10 years, the Nielsen Company specialized in surveys — mostly for industrial clients — and the going was rough. "We were broke, and it was a terribly risky thing," Arthur Nielsen reminisced in a *New York Times* interview in 1967. "I had a mortgage on everything, and there wasn't another dime in the world that we could beg or borrow." Even so, in 1933 — at the nadir of the Depression — he started a new service, the Nielsen Drug Index, which would become the mainspring for his company's growth in the future.

Developed for package goods manufacturers, NDI was based on what was then a novel idea: Draw a sample of drugstores and then visit them periodically to develop, through audits of purchase invoices and shelf stock, a measure of unit sales. This was logical for Mr. Nielsen since both his parents were accountants. (His father was manager of the general accounting division of Quaker Oats Company, Chicago.)

These store movements data, when projected, provided a measure of category size and a record of sales velocity, which then could be related to marketing efforts. In the process, he produced an exciting new concept: share of market. This turned marketing into a horse race, and only Mr. Nielsen had the scorecard. More marketing decisions, expenditures, and careers have been influenced by that single statistic — share of market — than any other.

A companion service, the Nielsen Food Index, was started seven months after NDI, and since then, the adaptation of the index methodology to other store categories and the expansion of index services in foreign countries have been the main thrust of the Nielsen company. Today, ACN Index services has over 1,500 corporate clients in 23 countries.

Mr. Nielsen was a pioneer in oversees expansion; he launched his first foreign subsidiary in Great Britain in 1939, a bold move for a man who had the personal reputation of being ultraconservative in business and politics. In the years since, many U.S. research companies have followed his lead in exporting research expertise.

In developing the index services, Mr. Nielsen did several other things that, in their day, were innovative. He paid retailers for their "cooperation." He sold his service on a syndicated basis, with all clients getting basically the same data — and sharing the cost. He asked clients to sign continuous contracts with stiff terms, which gave his business stability. (In later years, he added an escalation clause to these contracts with automatic rate increases geared to the Consumer Price Index; a good part of the company's revenue growth record has been a result of that clause.)

Mr. Nielsen made store panels available for experimentation back in 1933, thus foreseeing the need for "test marketing." And he decided early on to use full-time, salaried employees — mostly college graduates — as field auditors. This cadre produced the managers needed for his company's rapid growth, and hundreds of men so trained have sifted into marketing positions in the package goods industry.

Into Broadcast

Mr. Nielsen also was one of the pioneers in broadcast audience measurements, starting in 1936 when radio set ownership grew to the level where there was commercial interest. His Nielsen Radio Index service brought the "share-of-market" concept to the communications industry.

Mr. Nielsen's innovative approach to audience measures was something you would have expected from a man trained as an electrical engineer; his famous Audimeter was a mechanical device that could be wired to sets to continuously record time on and station tuned.

This was one of several mechanical devices that intrigued Mr. Nielsen. He also developed the Gas-Oil Recordimeter to attach to automobiles which automatically recorded purchases of gasoline and oil, and the House Recordimeter, an in-home device through which housewives could record their purchases (Mr. Nielsen's answer to mail diary panels).

The years 1946 to 1955 were tough on audience research services, and the Nielsen Company reportedly lost $13,000,000. But, as Mr. Nielsen said to me over lunch in 1969, "Think of the free advertising." The radio service was discontinued in 1964, but by then the Nielsen name had become a household word because of his TV ratings service — and a cussword among entertainers who were canceled because of low ratings.

It was in these years that Mr. Nielsen started to receive professional accolades: in 1951, the Paul D. Converse Award from the American Marketing Association for contributions to the science of marketing; in 1963, the Parlin Memorial Award for "demonstrated meritorious achievement in marketing and advertising research"; and in 1966, citation as Advertising Man of the Year by the International Advertising Association.

Mr. Nielsen's business skill is best exemplified by his company's long-term policy of investment in tangible assets, rare for a service company. Today the company owns outright 11 buildings totaling 557,500 sq. ft.; these, plus land values, are carried on the books — at cost less depreciation — at $37,700,000, which is just a fraction of their probable market value today. Most are located in what are now prime industrial park developments where Mr. Nielsen was often among the first to buy in.

Concurrent with his professional growth, Mr. Nielsen achieved an enviable record in the world of tennis, a sport he took up while attending Morton High School in Cicero, Ill. At the University of Wisconsin, he was captain of the varsity tennis team for three years and continued to play in tournaments through his advanced years. He twice won the national father-son doubles championship in the Veterans Division (over 45), and once, the national father-daughter hardcourt championship. In 1971, Mr. Nielsen was elected to the National Lawn Tennis Hall of Fame.

In his prime, Mr. Nielsen worked 60 to 70 hours a week, and his employees were used to being bombarded with his memos, which were long and detailed. Many were drafted in the back seat of his eight-passenger blue Fleetwood Cadillac, which — complete with blue shag rug — was equipped as a moving office. Mr. Nielsen traveled by ship as he thought flying was dangerous, and the trunk of his car was equipped to carry the voluminous files he took on his long auto trips through countries he toured in the process of building his overseas empire. He was proud of his car burglar alarm which, said Mr. Nielsen, "makes a noise that would scare the gizzard out of you."

Mr. Nielsen had the reputation of being a supersalesman, which dated back to his personal selling of Index Services in the 1930s.

I can personally attest to his skills in this area. In 1969, I called on Mr. Nielsen to solicit advertising for a new research magazine, *The Analyst*. He invited me to lunch in the private dining room off his office, and I found that — in addition to being most attentive to my plans — Mr. Nielsen had prepared for my visit; he had some thoughts that he wanted to sell me, which he did most effectively. On the way out, he said that the Nielsen Company would buy an ad in every issue of *The Analyst* as long as it was published simply because "it's a good thing for the industry."

The remarkable impression the man made during that brief encounter continues today. One unfortunate aspect of his career is that so few research people outside his company had the experience of knowing him personally.

Mr. Nielsen is survived by his wife, Gertrude; two sons, Arthur C. Nielsen, Jr., chairman of the board, and Philip R., vice president of the company, and three daughters.

Chapter 9

Eight Trends that Shaped an Industry

This material was first presented in a speech I made to the national American Marketing Association Research Conference at the Fairmont Hotel in New Orleans, on September 10, 1980. An edited version appeared as an article in an Advertising Age *section devoted to the research industry on October 20, 1980.*

Some of the details differ now, but the main points seem to be just as relevant today — maybe more so.

Research Trends

For over 15 years now I've spent a considerable amount of time documenting what goes on in this nebulous, sprawling, growing phenomenon called "the research industry."

From this observation I have identified eight major trends — or forces, if you will — that have, at least in my opinion, shaped the industry's development. These trends help explain what has happened, how our industry has changed over that time. But, perhaps more important, a review of what has happened facilitates a look into the future, a better understanding of what lies ahead in the 1980s.

This morning I'd like to talk with you a bit about these eight trends, and then, at the end, I'll close with some prophecies about how these trends may wend their way through the years ahead.

Before getting into specifics, let's start with a generalization: if you study the development of the advertising agency industry in the United States, I think you'll find — as I have — many parallels between that and the growth of the research industry. But there's a 10-year lead-lag relationship. In short, you'll learn a lot about where we're going if you look at where they've been.

1. We Come to See the Elephant

You've probably all heard the old saw about the group of blind men trying to describe an elephant. One touched the elephant's trunk, and got one impression. Another touched the elephant's legs, and he got another impression. And so on. None of them could visualize the whole and see how it all fit together.

That's the way the research community was when I started to study and ask questions 15 years ago. Survey people saw surveys — but that was about all. Store audit people saw audits — but that was about all. And so on through all segments of the industry — copy testing, diary panels, audience research, and so on.

Most research people were myopic: they had little or no intellectual curiosity about how other segments of their industry operated, or what they contributed to problem solving. So, if one had a survey background, the answer to every problem was a survey, and so on.

This situation, I believe, has changed considerably in the past 15 years. There are three reasons:

1.   Some research suppliers, to expand their business, either bought, or started, services in what to them were new areas. In the process, they started to get educated, to get more perspective. More important, they started to talk up other data collection techniques instead of talking them down.

2.   Clients became more systems oriented, and it became common to find data series from, say, two or three outside sources being amalgamated with internal data — such as factory shipments — to come up with a composite picture of what was going on in the pipeline and market place. This forced some suppliers, at least, to become familiar with all the inputs and how they could fit together for a better understanding, or perspective.

3.   Some suppliers made available fully integrated systems, and more clients started to see that one plus one could equal three. Ad Tel is an illustration of what I'm talking about; So is John Malek's new operation, Information Resources.

The end result is that, over time, more and more research practitioners, and their clients, embraced integration of data and, in the process, became less provincial. In that respect, they've become more problem-solving oriented — and less technique oriented. However, there's still a long way to go — there are still plenty of technique-blind people in the research industry.

2. Research Goes Public

There are two ways to look at this phenomenon. Let's start with the most literal.

If you look at the 23 largest U.S. research organizations that I identified in *Advertising Age* last May, you'll see that 78 percent of their aggregate revenues are accounted for by organizations that are either (1) publicly owned or (2) a wholly-owned subsidiary of a publicly listed corporation.

I have the impression that there are still many people on your side of the desk who do not realize that, for instance, when they talk with a representative of SAMI, they are really dealing with an employee of Time Incorporated. Or that a Chilton Research Service representative is really an employee of the American Broadcasting Company. Or that a person from Yankelovich, Skelly & White really works for Reliance Corporation. Or that a study purchased from Research Information Center — Hilda Barnes's operation out in Phoenix — is really being purchased from Greyhound. When you deal with Arbitron, you're really dealing with Control Data. And so on.

In times past, people like you bought research from dinky little companies that were financially insecure and highly dependent upon you. Today, chances are you are buying from organizatons that are as large and financially stable as the one you work for.

This has several ramifications:

1. These representatives have benefits — retirement programs, medical programs, etc. — personal security that was very rare in research service firms 15 years ago.

2. They are governed, to some degree, by corporate policies that dictate such things as billing procedures and legal restraints. I am very sensitive to this; for over six years I ran a research subsidiary of Dun & Bradstreet. When we wanted to deal with an employee, we had a two-inch thick manual from the corporate personnel department that stipulated what we could, and could not do. Among other things, we couldn't give highly productive employees a year-end bonus to reward them.

3. These corporate parents can supply what to the research industry are relatively high infusions of investment capital and technical support. I think the SAMI organization is a prime example of this. It took about ten years and about $14 million of Time, Inc. money before that operation saw black ink, and even that would

not have been possible but for the huge computer installation Time, Inc. already had set up in Chicago to handle subscription fulfillments. Now — granted — that's an extreme example — but it does underscore the impact public ownership can have on the research industry.

4.   The men who manage these publicly owned or subsidiary organizations are forced to be businessmen first, researchers second. Their mission is to deliver an acceptable bottom line to the owners. And that implies all sorts of things, which I won't belabor.

So, that's the literal side of the research industry's going public. The other facet is attitudinal. Put simply, research organizations — buyer and seller — in times past were very secretive about their doings. In the past 15 years, this has changed enormously. I think my writings in *Advertising Age* mirror that change, and as a result, more and more research practitioners have come to have a better understanding, and perspective, of what their industry is all about. And they've come to recognize common problems — field labor costs, legal restrictions, postage rates, etc.

3. The Urge to Merge

Closely akin to point 2 is the profusion of mergers and acquisitions over the past 15 years. There have been, literally, dozens of such financial transactions among research service firms. Some properties have turned over two and three times. Many of these deals have turned out to be disastrous for the buyer — or the seller — or both. In that sense, they have weakened the industry.

Some of this propensity to sell out has been due to the retirement plans of elderly owners. Others have been inspired by a desire to become a stronger, more diversified competitor in the market place. Some have been out of financial necessity.

In many cases, the purchaser is in a position to infuse development capital into the research firms it acquires, as we noted before. In that sense, they have strengthened the industry.

In the end, perhaps, all this churn will lead to a more stable industry — but in the meantime, it has also resulted in a lot of career concern for research practitioners.

4. Research Has Less "Character"

When I started this speech, you'll remember, I said that there were many interesting parallels between the advertising agency business and our own.

Most advertising agencies, if you look back, were founded by colorful, dynamic people — usually from the creative side. Much the same thing was true of the research industry. There were all sorts of personable characters who brought prominence to research, fought the good fight; in many respects, they were showmen. Politz, Dichter, Henry Brenner, Sam Barton, Pierre Martineau, Bill Simmons — I could go on and on. Even Art Nielsen, Sr., was a dynamic showman in his day.

But, as is pretty much true in the advertising agency business, these innovative pioneers have passed from the scene. In their place — partly because of the public ownership we discussed previously — we now find relatively bland businessmen running major research organizatons. They are not, generally, imaginative, innovative, or spell-binding presenters. What they are is exactly what you get in a maturing industry — conservative businessmen who are much more likely to know about accounting practices than sampling theory; much more likely to know about computers than psychology; more likely to read balance sheets than Margaret Mead. Their counterparts on the buyer's side of the desk tend to be good corporate soldiers . . . 20-year men interested in not rocking the boat.

The pioneers disturbed us; they made us think. They financed new data collection techniques because they were interested in the possible findings, and the profit potential was secondary. Some of them darn near wrecked their companies in the process. Art Nielsen started the index services in the depths of the Great Depression; Sam Barton tore MRCA apart with his first menu census, which was a financial disaster.

In sum, they gave our industry a dynamic nature, a vibrance that over the past 15 years has pretty much ebbed away. In its place, we've gotten the MBA. I, for one, miss the excitement.

5. Form Over Substance

Computer technology, no doubt, is the one thing that has most altered the nature of our industry over the past 15 years. I'm particularly conscious of this because, when I started out, a researcher had to know how to wire an IBM 101 statistical sorter to get anything done.

There's no reason to belabor what the computer has meant in terms of lowering costs, speed, flexibility, and statistical techniques. All to the good — with one exception: with the computer came a new breed of "researcher," one who was, it seems, more concerned with form than substance. Since they were so far removed from the data collection phase, and even further removed from the reality — the consumer who supplied the input — they couldn't really comprehend GIGO — garbage in, garbage out. They didn't want to hear it; they seemed to be in a trance — through the computer, they could restructure and identify subterranean currents in the data. In a word, elegant software could make a silk purse from a sow's ear.

The conceptualization inherent in their techniques snowed a lot of people and — to be fair — some new ground was broken.

But the main thing, in my opinion, was that emphasis shifted from getting closer to the flesh and blood consumer, the walking and talking reality from whence knowledge stemmed, to esoteric data manipulation. Many of those expensive Holy Grails are still sitting on window sills around the country yellowed from the sun and garnished with dead flies. Largely, they were the creations of people who had never been in a supermarket for observational purposes, or who had never conducted an interview in the field.

6. Rapid Growth

No one knows for sure, but based on my annual analysis of the performance of the largest U.S. research organizations, it seems reasonable to say that the research industry — in terms of revenues — was growing at an annual rate of 19 percent during the 1970s.

When you take inflation into account and look at real growth, you get a different picture. "Real growth" was running in the neighborhood of 15 to 17 percent in the early 1970s, but it slowed down to 12 percent in the late 1970s, and it's probably closer to 5 percent today. Showing signs of topping off, if you will. But, of course, that growth is on a bigger base.

Be that as it may, the research industry has been a steady boom industry over the past 15 years.

Here's a little barometer of that — you are all probably familiar with the so-called "Green Book" published by the New York chapter of the AMA. It's a directory of research houses and allied services. When the first Green Book was published in 1962, there were 46 listings. By 1974, this had grown to 522 listings. The 1980 edition has 840 listings.

Now, this is misleading in many respects — one of which is that many of those additional listings are the result of research companies' opening up branch offices, or subsidiaries, and buying a listing for each. But that's an indicator of growth, too — or maybe we should call it sprawl.

There are many reasons for this rapid growth, but I'd like to underscore just three.

1. New services tend to expand the market. I don't mean to pick on SAMI this morning, but there's a conspicuous example of what I'm talking about. SAMI revenues in 1979 exceeded $54 million. I estimate that about one-half of that was at the expense of the Nielsen index services; the rest was found money — additional money attracted to the research industry by what was perceived as a valuable new data series.

To some degree, I think almost any really innovative new service performs the same function. It seems likely that scanner-based systems, when they are on-line and smoothed out, will expand the business too.

2. More industries have embraced research as a permanent fact of business life. Time permitting, we could cite numerous examples — banking, retailing, political opinion research, research sponsored by news media, and so on. This expansion has gone quickly because new entrants could buy people and adopt techniques developed by the package goods industry which, for so many years, underwrote most of the marketing research innovation in the United States.

3. The selling of research services is much more methodical and professional today than 15 years ago. The monies spent for brochures, advertising, travel, and salespersons have increased by several fold.

7. Machined Research

Just think of the explosion of automated, machine-based data collection in the past 15 years. UPC scanners, CRT interviewing, WATS networks, interactive systems with direct consumer feedback, physiological measuring devices, and so on, and so on. Speed, lower cost, more control — these have been the order of the day, the driving force. And, let's face it, technological advances have a certain romance about them — especially to clients, it seems.

Aside from the mechanical considerations, I think this development has had a subtle, but very important impact on attitudes within the research community. It goes something like this: the research industry has — and this trend seems to be accelerating — become less humanistic. How a consumer feels, senses, breathes, burps, and whims gets pushed further into the background; instead, researchers are increasingly concerned with static on transmission lines, numbers of dialings, faster printers, and other such impersonal phenomena.

Ironically, concurrently, the consumer is showing increasing signs of being turned off by the whole process of being interviewed.

Research has become, more and more, a game of hide and go seek. So, instead of an increasingly closer rapport between researchers and their constituents, the consumer, there seems to be an ever widening schism.

Automation may be a great achievement for cost and efficiency — but it may also result in a loss of understanding, which after all is the name of the game.

8. Do It Yourself

The eighth, and final, trend I'd like to discuss today is the growing self-sufficiency by large research users. There are several prominent examples — General Foods, General Mills, Procter & Gamble, Pillsbury, and some advertising agencies. They have developed large, well-staffed internal research organizations. I can't document it — but I have the impression that this phenomenon has accelerated over the past 15 years. We do have good estimates, for instance, that Procter & Gamble spends nearly $10 million in-house for do-it-yourself consumer research. The estimate for General Mills is $6 million. Both General Foods and Quaker Oats spend in excess of $5 million in-house.

There are obviously several reasons for this — save money, faster turnaround, confidentiality, utilization of internal facilities (like WATS lines), more control, proprietary techniques — to name a few.

In the process, of course, such do-it-yourselfers become more sophisticated as to costs, field techniques, etc. — and, theoretically, that should make them more knowing buyers when they do buy on the outside. Also — and I trust this is obvious — they have established a precedent that may well be followed by others.

So, Where Do We Go Next?

From what I've said so far, I assume you're getting the picture of a large, growing, increasingly conspicuous industry — with a strong bent towards technology. In many respects, it's becoming a mature, capital-intensive industry.

Now, I'd like to close with a review of each of the eight major trends I've discussed and make some predictions of things to come. These are nothing more than one man's opinion, and later I'd be very interested in your own appraisal.

1. **We come to see the elephant.** There will be more of this, which really means fewer specialists and more generalists. There will be more of a problem-solving orientation, less of a data collection technique orientation.

2. **Research goes public.** This will continue. Just recently, there have been three new cases: Elrick & Lavidge being acquired by Equifax; Rogers National Research being acquired by Maritz, Inc.; and Automated Marketing Systems of Chicago buying 20 percent of Information Resources, Inc. — plus an option to buy the balance in 1984.

3. **The urge to merge.** There has been a trend toward a concentration of power in the research industry, and to many that is the

road to survival. This trend will continue, if not accelerate. The squeeze will be on the mid-sized ($1 to $5 million) operation, many of which are poorly managed and strapped for working capital.

4. **Research has less "character".** In the advertising agency business, we saw many of the leading firms get very large and institutionalized; many went public.

   And we've also seen a counter-trend: a rush by some clients to embrace the boutiques — feisty, irreverent, and exciting collections of creative mustangs.

   I think, in time, you'll see a similar counter-trend in the research industry — a hungering by top management for fewer studies — but hand-tailored, thoughtful, craftsman-like projects by experienced professionals. And money will be no object. Quality of understanding will become more important than quantity. This will lead to a resurgence of small, highly personalized firms that consult as much as execute research projects.

5. **Form over substance.** I think there will be greater realization that exotic data manipulation is the province of technocrats — not innovative marketers. The emphasis will shift back to personal involvement with the consumer — standing in a supermarket all day to watch what happens, doing the pilot studies personally, construction of humanistic questionnaires instead of those that are designed, primarily, to facilitate data processing.

6. **Rapid growth.** I think we'll continue to have real growth — mostly because well-funded service firms will develop helpful new information products that will expand the market. But most of the growth, I believe, will not be in traditional research services; instead it will center on "information systems" data banks.

7. **Machined research.** No doubt, this will continue in the near future — scanner-developed data are an example — but eventually researchers and their employers will sense that instead of getting closer to the consumer, too much technology, in fact, is building a wall. Then there will be a counter reaction — the seeking of humanistic approaches to research.

8. **Do it yourself.** I think this will accelerate — partly because of cost considerations, but mostly because the integration of confidential internal information can add greatly to the value of a research study.

In the end, however, what you people in this room think and do over the next ten years will have a considerable impact on how our industry evolves. I urge you to be movers, not followers.

I think that in the past, too many research leaders have just assumed that the facts speak for themselves. Not so. Researchers must speak for the facts.

Chapter 10

Top Thirty U.S. Research Companies

Back in 1971 when I first started to write for Advertising Age, *the editor, Rance Crain, asked why there was no annual summary of how the top firms did, comparable to AA's U.S. Agency Income Profiles. I answered that that would be very difficult since so many of the large firms were privately held and very secretive about their financials. Moreover, there was a definitional problem: Exactly what type of firms should be included in such a research industry overview?*

However, there was a real need for such an article. Hardly anyone within the industry (or outside) had the vaguest idea about the size of other obviously major firms, and some — notably Gallup and Harris — had a reputation far larger than their size because of the prominence of their syndicated newspaper columns. Other, much larger firms were virtually unknown away from their immediate client base. Further, if we had an accurate year-to-year record of how the major firms were growing in revenue, collectively that would provide an important piece of marketing news: a barometer of the industry's growth in the United States (and, indeed, it was growing very rapidly in those days).

Rance kept on the subject, and finally, in the Advertising Age *of July 18, 1974, I published the first such listing, which described just the 10 largest firms. Moreover, to do that, I first had to define what type of organization qualified. Hence, this definition:*

> *A for-profit corporate identity which has as its main enterprise the development of proprietary measures in the field of marketing, public attitudes, media consumption, or advertising stimuli, that are basically related to the sale of goods or services. This definition includes, at one extreme, the measures of market size and share of market, and at the other, the perceptions that might be gained from one, small focused group interview.*

That first listing drew a lot of very critical mail. People argued with my definition and, more specifically, with the implied notion that annual dollar volume equated with quality of service. Reading back now, underlying much of that criticism was a very human reaction, namely, "Hey, you left me out!"

Mr. Crain urged me to do it again in 1975, and that listing too was based on just 10 firms. However, other events were starting to shape this annual review. One was that some large research organizations went public, and others were acquired by larger, public companies, which had a different attitude towards public disclosure. In any case, the listings in 1976, '77, and '78 were based on 20 firms. In 1979 this went to 23, in '80 to 25, in '81 to 28, and finally in 1981 to 30 firms. The 1982 review, which was published in Advertising Age *on May 23, 1983, was showcased in its own portfolio section with a descriptive cover; the annual research company listing had, nine years after it was started, finally received the same status that advertising agencies had enjoyed through the years.*

More important, with 30 companies listed and the detail of disclosure increasing every year, the annual review had really come to perform the goal set back in 1974: It was a workably accurate barometer of the industry's growth. In fact, these trend data overshadow the individual company reports now.

Another by-product of this annual listing was that the research industry's growth and size could be compared to that of a closely allied industry, advertising agencies. Further, the size of leading research firms could be compared with that of large advertising agencies, which tend to be much more prominent. (See Table 10-1.) Lo and behold, often a relatively obscure research firm was larger!

There follows what has become the definitive Who's Who of the American research industry, circa 1983.

Overview

The U.S. marketing/advertising research industry ended 1982 — an unsettled year characterized by numerous acquisitions — with a 10.3 percent increase in revenues over '81, according to this, the 9th annual review of industry performance compiled exclusively for *Advertising Age.*

After adjustment for inflation — which was 6.1 percent in '82, according to the U.S. Department of Labor's Consumer Price Index-U, monthly average — the industry had a so-called "real growth" rate of 4.2 percent, slightly better than the comparable figure of 3.4 percent in '81 and 4 percent in '80, but still way below the heydays of 1975-78 when real growth exceeded 10 percent every year. (See Figure 10-1.)

Table 10-1   How the Top 30 U.S. Research Agencies Compare to the Top 30 U.S. Advertising Agencies

	Top 30 U.S. Advertising Agencies*	Top 30 U.S. Research Agencies
Revenues — 1982 (add 000)		
Worldwide	$4,358.9	$1,121.2
U.S. only	2,705.2	1,019.7
Growth rate (1982 over '81)		
Worldwide	+12.2%	+10.3%
U.S. only	+16.6%	+15.8%

* Source: *Advertising Age* U.S. Agency Income Profiles, 1983, edition — 3/16/83.

The top 30 U.S. firms listed in Table 10-2 in 1982 had gross worldwide revenues of $1,121,200,000, with 29.7 percent (or $332.5 million) coming from operations outside the United States. As usual, the giant A. C. Nielsen Company, with research revenues of $433.1 million, or 38.6 percent of the total, dominated the list — and its relatively weak performance in '82 leveraged down the total industry's performance. In the years 1975-81, ACN averaged 20 percent growth per year; in 1982, this fell to 5.2 percent, mostly due to a drop-off from store audit operations.

ACN's performance, alone one of the main "findings" of this year's analysis, is almost equalled by the profusion of acquisitions that took place in calendar '82; the top 30 firms alone acquired nine other research organizations during the year, and this furthered the trend toward a concentration of ownership within the U.S. research industry.

So, to make sure these acquisitions did not unrealistically inflate the industry's growth rate, the revenue increases (decreases) for individual firms were calculated as follows: Assuming company "A" bought company "B" sometime during 1982, the revenues of both companies for all of 1982 were combined for the 1982 listing, and then compared to the combined revenues of both in 1981 to produce a rate of change, be it gain or loss. The specifics of these acquisitions and the organizations involved are contained in the 30 individual company profiles that come later in this analysis.

U.S. Revenues Up 14.9 Percent

The total industry figures are influenced greatly by revenues coming from outside the United States, and most of that is concentrated in the two worldwide conglomerates, A. C. Nielson and IMS International, which alone account for $323.9 million of overseas volume. If U.S.-only revenues for the top 30 are considered, they collectively had a 14.9 percent increase in '82; for overseas revenues alone, it is just slightly less than 1 percent. Part of this situation — maybe the major part — is the result of a weakening of foreign currencies

Table 10-2   1982 Revenue Record* 30 Leading U.S. Research Firms

Rank	Research Organization	Research revenues (Add 000,000)	% Change vs. 1981	Research revenues from outside U.S. (Add 000,000)
1	A. C. Nielsen Company	$ 433.1	+ 5.2	$242.1
2	IMS International, Inc.	124.8	+ 8.3	81.8
3	SAMI	85.0	+ 17.1	—
4	The Arbitron Ratings Company	80.3	+ 20.9	—
5	Burke Marketing Services, Inc.	52.1	+ 18.9	1.4
6	Market Facts, Inc.	25.4	0	—
7	Audits & Surveys, Inc.	22.5	**	—
8	NFO Research, Inc.	22.0	+ 14.0	—
9	Marketing and Research Counselors	21.9	+ 21.7	—
10	The NPD Group	21.5	+ 20.1	—
11	Maritz Market Research, Inc.	18.5	− 2.1	—
12	Westat, Inc.	17.3	+ 8.8	—
13	Elrick and Lavidge, Inc.	16.9	+ 15.8	—
14	ASI Market Research, Inc.	16.3	+ 9.4	0.7
15	Chilton Research Services	16.2	+ 6.6	—
16	Yankelovich, Skelly & White, Inc.	13.4	+ 3.9	—
17	Walker Research, Inc.	12.6	+ 7.8	—
18	Information Resources, Inc.	12.3	+109.5	—
19	Louis Harris and Associates, Inc.	12.1	+ 19.8	3.8
20	The Ehrhart-Babic Group	11.9	+ 1.7	0.1
21	Data Development Corp.	11.8	+ 5.4	—
22	Winona Research, Inc.	11.3	+ 11.9	—
23	Opinion Research Corp.	10.2	+ 24.4	—
24	Harte-Hanks Marketing Services Group	9.6	+ 2.8	—
25	Decision Center, Inc.	8.4	+ 21.7	—
26	McCollum/Spielman/& Company, Inc.	7.1	+ 16.4	—
27	Starch INRA Hooper, Inc.	7.0	+ 10.1	1.4
28	Market Opinion Research	6.7	+ 43.4	0.7
29	National Analysts	6.6	− 1.0	—
30	Custom Research, Inc.	6.4	+ 36.2	—
		$1,121.2	+ 10.3**	$332.5

* Total revenues, which include non-research activities for some companies are significantly higher. This information is given in the individual company profiles in the main article.

** No new input was received from A&S for 1982; therefore it was not included in calculating industry growth from year to year.

**Figure 10-1   U.S. Research Industry Year-to-Year Revenue
Growth Rate Total — and Adjusted for Inflation
1975-1982**

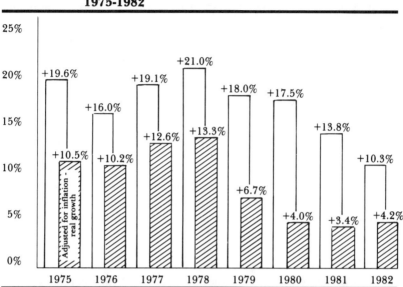

vis-à-vis the U.S. dollar, which tends to dilute overseas revenues when they are converted into dollars for a consolidated financial statement. Just the opposite was true in previous years, and to the extent it was, the growth of the U.S. research industry — including its overseas revenues — was unrealistically overstated.

Be that as it may, of the 14.9 percent increase in U.S. revenues only, the lion's share, expressed in dollar volume, can be attributed to three sources: the TV audience measurement services of Arbitron and the Media Research Group of A. C. Nielsen (spurred by the proliferation of meter-based audience measurement systems at the local market level), and the spectacular growth of Information Resources, Inc., the Chicago-based firm that operates the BehaviorScan system in four mini-markets for controlled testing of advertising, merchandising, and new product efforts. IRI made more news in early 1983 by floating a public stock issue that could bring in close to $25 million for expansion efforts (two new markets to be added in '83).

A Public Industry

Of the top 30's collective revenue in '82, only 20 percent is attributable to organizations that are privately held; the balance comes from organizations that are either publicly owned or subsidiaries of publicly owned companies (as of 1982).

The profiles of 1982's top 30 companies that follow document their total revenues (which in many cases exceed their research-only revenues), ownership, changes in organization and top management in 1982-83, and expansion plans for the balance of 1983. For many of the 30, 1982 was an extraordinary year — and collectively, the U.S. industry underwent considerable change.

Company Profiles

A. C. NIELSEN COMPANY — Northbrook, Illinois

Public company traded over the counter. Founded in 1923. Research revenues in 1982 were $433.1 million, up 5.2 percent over '81.

For the 12 months ended November 30, 1982, the world's largest marketing/advertising research organization has gross revenues of $654.2 million. Of that, 66.2 percent — or $433.1 million — was from research operations in 25 countries. To put ACN's diversification efforts into perspective, research activities accounted for 72.6 percent of ACN's total revenues in 1978, and that percentage has gone down each year since.

Also, ACN's research-only revenues of $433.1 million in '82 were $56.5 million more than the world gross income of the largest U.S. advertising agency, Young & Rubicam.

Be that as it may, 1982 was an unaccustomed downer for ACN; the research-only growth rate of 5.2 percent compares with a yearly average of close to 20 percent for the years 1975-81. Moreover, of the growth in '82 — $21.4 million — 78.5 percent was attributable to the ACN Media Research Group, which specializes in national and local market TV audience measurements. That left the Marketing Research Group, which specializes in syndicated and custom audits of product movement at retail, with a growth rate of only 1.4 percent, or $4.96 million.

Put another way, ACN's overseas revenues in '82 (basically syndicated store audit services in 24 countries) were down by nearly $2 million in '82, while U.S. revenues were up 13.8 percent.

As for new developments in the research activities of ACN, here are some noted in the address Arthur C. Nielsen, Jr., chairman and CEO, made to shareholders on February 14, 1983:

- A new addition to the corporate headquarters in Northbrook, Ill.

- The testing of a so-called "people meter" for possible use in TV audience measurements. This attachment allows the viewer to enter his demographics automatically while viewing a particular channel. Said Mr. Nielsen, "If the test proves successful we would expect to manufacture and install these recorders in homes throughout the United States."

- A device called NIAT, which is now being used on an experimental basis. It enables field auditors to enter data into a memory, which at night can be transmitted via telephone to ACN production center computers.

- Increasing national TV audience sample from 1,200 to 1,700 meter-equipped households.

President of ACN is N. Eugene Harden, 48, a graduate of Lawrence University. Henry Burk, 56, is president of ACN's Marketing Research Group, and James D. Lyon, 47, is president of the Media Research Group. Arthur C. Nielsen, Jr., 63, is chairman and chief executive officer.

IMS INTERNATIONAL, INC.
New York, New York

Public corporation traded over the counter. Founded in 1954. Research revenues in 1982 were $124.8 million, up 8.3 percent over '81.

Of IMS's total revenues ($226.9 million), 55 percent — or $124.8 million — came from its Market Research Division subsidiaries in 57 countries. (In 1977, 74 percent of IMS's total revenues came from research activities; that percentage has dropped each year since as the result of diversification activities.)

Research revenues in the United States (through its subsidiary, IMS America, Ambler, Pa.) were $43 million, or 34.5 percent of the total; that's an increase of 13.2 percent over '81. Overseas research revenues of $81.8 million, in contrast, were up only 5.9 percent, a situation due largely to the strengthening of the U.S. dollar vis-à-vis most foreign currencies; that tended to dilute foreign revenues as they were converted to dollars for the company's consolidated report.

IMS, as in years past, continued to obtain almost all its market research business from the worldwide pharmaceutical/medical and health care industries, where its position is akin to that enjoyed by the A. C. Nielsen Company in the package goods industries. IMS research activities consist mainly of syndicated audits of product movement through panels of doctors, drug stores, hospitals, medical laboratories, nursing homes, etc. Emphasis in recent years has been on the development of on-line access to IMS data bases via a system called MIDAS.

There are about 2,000 full-time, salaried employees in the Market Research Division of IMS.

Chairman, president, and chief executive officer of IMS is Lars H. Ericson, 48.

SAMI — New York, New York

Wholly owned subsidiary of Time, Inc. Founded in 1966. Research revenues for 1982 were estimated at $85 million, up about 17 percent over '81.

The basic activity of SAMI is to amalgamate warehouse withdrawal data to produce continuous movement data on thousands of individual package goods items sold through food stores, separately for each of 48 market areas, three of which were added to the system during 1982: Charleston/Huntington, Quad Cities, and Wichita. In toto, these 48 SAMI market areas represent about 84.3 percent of total U.S. ACV.

Regarding 1982 revenues, SAMI says that revenues of their companion SARDI service were up 36 percent over 1981, and revenues from the Segmentation and SAMSCAN services more than doubled over the year before.

SAMI also reports that currently extensive modification of their computer software systems is being carried out with an eye towards putting the entire SAMI data base on-line.

There are 400 full-time, salaried employees located in three U.S. office locations.

President of SAMI is Carlyle C. Daniel, 52, a graduate of Lynchburg College.

THE ARBITRON RATINGS COMPANY
New York, New York

Wholly-owned subsidiary of Control Data Corporation. Founded in 1949. Revenues in 1982 were $80.3 million, up 20.9 percent over '81.

ARC's basic business is local market measurements of radio and TV audiences, mostly via mail diaries. In '82, ARC conducted surveys in 256 radio markets (accounting for about $37 million in revenue) and 210 TV markets (accounting for about $43 million). In addition to existing meter-equipped samples in New York, Chicago, Los Angeles, and San Francisco, ARC opened up meter TV measures in Philadelphia and Dallas in early '83. Meter service will be added in Washington, D.C., Detroit, and Miami during '83.

During '82, ARC developed U.S. AID, a national data base of 5,000 TV diary households for examining nationwide viewing patterns. Also, the company introduced PRIZM/AID, a computer-based system that combines radio and TV audience data with Claritas Corporation's PRIZM geodemographic life style information at the Zip Code level.

During 1983, ARC will begin surveying radio audiences 48 weeks rather than 44 weeks per year. Qualidata 1983, a study of product and media usage by radio listeners in 10 major markets, is scheduled to debut in mid-'83.

ARC has 811 full-time, salaried employees in seven U.S. offices.

ARC president is Theodore F. Shaker, 61, who is also a vice president of Control Data Corporation. He attended Colgate, Northwestern, and New York Universities.

BURKE MARKETING SERVICES, INC.
Cincinnati, Ohio

Employee-owned corporation. Founded in 1947. Research revenues in 1982 were $52.1 million, up 18.9 percent over '81.

The activities of this conglomerate are organized as follows: (1) Test Marketing Group, a unit recently formed by merging AdTel (TV campaign testing in controlled market labs) and Market Audits (retail store audits); (2) BASES, which specializes in market modeling; (3) Burke Marketing Research, which specializes in pre- and post-TV copy testing and custom survey research; (4) Professional Services, which conducts research educational seminars; (5) a wholly owned subsidiary, Burke Canada; (6) Burke International, a joint venture with the German firm, Infratest; and (7) Telcom Research, Inc., a firm specializing in physiological measures in reaction to advertising stimuli, which was acquired by BMSI in August, '82.

All told, there are 365 full-time, salaried employees in the BMSI organization, which includes 46 office locations — 11 for client service staffs, the balance for field data collection activities. About $1.4 million of the company's revenue in '82 came from outside the United States.

Chairman of BMSI is Jack E. Brown, 38; he attended the University of Cincinnati.

MARKET FACTS, INC. — Chicago, Illinois

Public company traded over the counter. Founded in 1946. Research revenues in 1982 were $25.4 million, almost exactly the same as in '81.

Of total Market Facts revenues of $26.2 million in '82, about 3 percent came from non-research activities. Also, not included in these volumes are those of a partly owned subsidiary, Market Facts of Canada, which has annual revenues of about $2.4 million.

MF's U.S. activities include: (1) the Consumer Mail Panel (135,000 households); (2) Marketest Store Audit Services, seven permanent market setups for controlled store tests and test marketing; (3) five shopping mall facilities; (4) WATS telephone interviewing centers with 90 stations; and (5) focus group facilities. There are 714 full-time employees (429 of whom are salaried), located in 19 office locations, including the National Telephone Center in Evanston, Illinois, and an Operations Headquarters in Oak Park, Illinois.

In late '82, MF announced a new organization — Marketing Research Services Group, directing all the company's marketing efforts; a general manager heading all MF operating and administrative activities (including data collection and processing); and a president of Market Facts Ventures Groups, which has been formed to design and introduce new products and services.

President and chief operating officer of MF, as of December, 1982, is Verne B. Churchill, 50, who received his MBA from the Indiana University School of Business. Chairman and chief executive officer is David K. Hardin, 55, who received his MBA from the University of Chicago.

AUDITS & SURVEYS, INC.
New York, New York

Privately held corporation. Founded in 1953. Research revenues for 1981 estimated at $22.5 million; no updated information for 1982.

The Audits & Surveys organizaton in the United States includes the following business units: Survey Division (custom, ad hoc sample surveys); Test Audit Division (local market retail audits); National Total-Market Division (syndicated store audit programs, customized to the product class); Government Research Division (survey support for Federal agencies); Retail Census of Product Distribution (annual study of U.S. retail store population); and Selling-Areas Distribution Index (distribution checks in food, drug, discount, and variety stores). A separate company, CTIS (for Central Telephone Interviewing System), located in the Washington, D.C., area, offers field and tab service via a 125-station CATI system.

Not included are revenues from other organizations in which A&S or its principals have a financial position: A&S Latinamerica; Total-Market Index in Canada; Market Probe International; and Integrated Computer Systems, an EDP service bureau.

President of A&S is Richard L. Lysaker, 50, who is a graduate of the University of Minnesota. Solomon Dutka, 59, founder of A&S, is chairman; he received his PhD from Century University in Los Angeles.

NFO RESEARCH, INC. — Toledo, Ohio

Wholly owned subsidiary of AGB Research Ltd. Founded in 1946. Revenues in 1982 were $22 million, up 14 percent over '81.

In August 1982, NFO — via acquisition — became part of one of the world's largest research organizations, the London-based firm of AGB Research Ltd.

The 660 employees of NFO (of which 384 are full-time, salaried) are located in eight marketing branch offices and two production facilities — the home office in Toledo (to which a 55,000 sq. ft. addition was added in '82) and Greensboro, North Carolina.

NFO's main business is a fixed mail panel, which has been expanded to 220,000 households. Mail purchase panels, operated through NFO's TRAC syndicated research division, offer the following continuing studies: The Share of Intake Panel (consumption of all beverages); Men's Tailored Apparel Study; Home Furnishings Tracking Service — plus two new services added in 1982: Women's Tailored Apparel Study and the Personal Home Computer and Video Game Study.

NFO operates two WATS facilities for telephone interviewing — 160 stations in Toledo, 60 more in Greensboro.

Taking over as president and chief executive officer of NFO in mid-'82 was William E. Lipner, 36. He holds a BBA degree in business administration from the University of Toledo.

MARKETING AND RESEARCH COUNSELORS, INC. (M/A/R/C) — Dallas, Texas

Subsidiary of Allcom, Inc., a closely held public corporation. Founded in 1965. Revenues in 1982 were $21.9 million, up 21.7 percent over '81.

This survey research firm, which specializes in automated telephone interviewing, operates six WATS interviewing centers that have, in total, 215 stations. About 200 of these are operating on a M/A/R/C-developed Automatic Custom Research System (ACRS), a "state-of-the-art" computerized system that integrates interviewing with tabulating and is supported by a software library of 47 programs. The ACRS system is available to outsiders on a lease basis.

During '82, M/A/R/C sold five shopping center mall data collection facilities. Also in '82, M/A/R/C introduced a new service called the National Neighborhood Panel, which contains 26,000 Zip-Code clustered households in 22 geographical areas. These panel households are available for telephone, mail, or face-to-face interviewing. By 1984, says M/A/R/C, the panel will be expanded to 100,000 participating households in 25 markets.

M/A/R/C has 194 full-time, salaried employees, plus over 200 hourly staff professionals, located in nine U.S. offices.

President of M/A/R/C is Cecil B. (Bud) Phillips, 58, a graduate of Southern Methodist University.

THE NPD GROUP — Port Washington, New York

A group of privately held corporations under common ownership. Founded in 1967. Research revenues in 1982 were $21.5 million, up 20.1 percent over '81.

Listed as NPD Research, Inc., last year, this firm in the interim has undergone a reorganization, changed its name, and consolidated its New York area operations in a new, 93,000 sq. ft. headquarters building in the Roslyn North Industrial Park in the Long Island community of Port Washington.

The Group, which has 230 full-time, salaried employees, is now divisionalized as follows: NPD Research, Inc. (13,000-household national purchase panel specializing in package goods, plus more than 25 local-market panels with about 47,000 households); NPD Special Industry Services (purchase panels specializing in such product classes as toys/games, textile/apparel, petroleum products, sports equipment, and records/tapes); GDR/CREST Enterprises (panel reporting on meals eaten away from home); Home Testing Institute, Inc., a fixed mail panel currently being expanded to 130,000 households; and OPOC Computing Company, an EDP service bureau. (OPOC revenues are not included in the NPD research revenues above.)

A sales/service office of NPD is located in Rosemont, Illinois.

Founder, chairman and joint owner of NPD is Henry Brenner, 68. President, chief executive officer, and joint owner is Tod Johnson, 38; he holds an MSIA degree from Carnegie-Mellon University.

MARITZ MARKET RESEARCH, INC.
Fenton, Missouri

Wholly owned subsidiary of Maritz, Inc. Founded in 1973. Research revenues in 1982 were $18.5 million, down 2.1 percent from '82.

During 1982, MMRI made news — and broadened its business base — via the acquisition of three survey research firms: Quatra Marketing Research, Inc., in Minneapolis; Houlahan/Parker Marketing Research in Los Angeles; and Clare Brown Associates, Garwood, New Jersey.

The largest unit within MMRI is Quality Control Services, which — with 16 field offices — is believed to be the largest central location network in the United States. It is estimated that QCS accounts for about 40 percent of MMRI revenues.

In addition to working out of company headquarters in Fenton, MMRI staff performs custom and syndicated surveys through divisional offices in Detroit and Toledo. There are three WATS telephone survey facilities. In total, MMRI has 186 full-time, salaried employees.

President of MMRI is Paul E. Barnard, 53, who is a graduate of the University of Missouri. He reports to William H. Lewellen, group executive of the Maritz Research Services Group.

WESTAT — Rockville, Maryland

An employee-owned corporation. Founded in 1961. Revenues in 1982 were $17.3 million, up 8.8 percent over '81.

This survey research firm, which has 195 full-time, salaried employees, does over 90 percent of its work for agencies of the federal government. A new division, MARKETSTAT, was created in late '82 to expand the commercial business, concentrating on telephone-based studies.

Revenues come from a full range of survey research methodologies — personal, face-to-face, mail, and telephone interviewing, which includes a staff of about 325 phone interviewers and CATI capabilities.

President and chief executive officer at Westat is Joseph A. Hunt, 47, who has an MS degree from Massachusetts Institute of Technology. Edward C. Bryant, the founder of Westat, is chairman.

ELRICK AND LAVIDGE, INC. — Chicago, Illinois

Wholly owned subsidiary of Equifax, Inc. Founded in 1951. Research revenues in 1982 were $16.9 million in 1982, up 15.8 percent over '81.

E&L, a research firm specializing in both consumer and business-to-business surveys, moved up in this year's ranking due to the acquisition in late 1982 of Quick Test, Cornwells Heights, Pennsylvania.

Quick Test, with 11 shopping mall sites, is one of the largest central-location operations in the United States; it added about $5.8 million to E&L's volume. Subsequently, the 11 QT sites were merged in with four already operated by E&L to form a new, independent business unit, Quick Test Opinion Centers. Currently, microprocessors for interviewing are being installed in eight of the QTOC sites, which will make possible computer-controlled interviewing in several sites through one organization with common software and hardware.

Also, E&L has announced a new syndicated service called Multi-Call, which is based on face-to-face interviews in malls, with clients buying in on a question-by-question basis.

President of E&L is Robert J. Lavidge, 61, who has an MBA from the University of Chicago.

ASI MARKET RESEARCH, INC.
Los Angeles, California

Privately held corporation. Founded in 1962. Research revenues in 1982 were $16.3 million, up 9.4 percent over '81.

Total ASI revenues in '82 were $22.6 million, of which $16.3 million came from research activities, and $700,000 of that was attributable to a wholly owned subsidiary in Hong Kong.

ASI specializes in controlled audience pretesting and on-air (Recall Plus service) testing of TV commercials, custom research projects, testing of print ads, and focus groups. The company operates a 50-station WATS telephone center in Los Angeles.

ASI has 350 full-time, salaried employees.

President of ASI is Gerald Lukeman, 51, who is a graduate of Dartmouth College. Pierre Marquis, 56, a graduate of Boston University School of Law, is chairman.

CHILTON RESEARCH SERVICES
Radnor, Pennsylvania

Wholly owned subsidiary of American Broadcasting Company. Founded in 1957. Research revenues in 1982 were $16.2 million, up 6.6 percent over '81.

This custom survey-research firm has 158 full-time, salaried employees in two offices.

Chilton maintains one of the largest CATI installations in the United States — 125 stations, excluding two banks used only for the continuous AT&T Telsam studies.

New director of CRS, as of May, '83, is Gilbert Barrish, 43, a graduate of Temple University with a BS in economics.

YANKELOVICH, SKELLY AND WHITE, INC.
New York, New York

Wholly owned subsidiary of Reliance Group, Inc. Founded in 1958. Revenues in 1982 were $13.4 million, up 3.9 percent over '81.

This survey research firm does marketing and social research for industry, governmental agencies, and media — most notably *Time* and *Fortune* magazines. About 5 percent of YSW volume is from outside the United States.

Two of the company's most widely used services are (1) Monitor, tracking surveys of special social segments, and (2) Laboratory Test Market, a market simulation facility widely used by package goods manufacturers for new product appraisals. In mid-'82, YSW started to reorganize its basic survey activities (and staff) along client categories, namely: Consumer Marketing Group, New Products Group, Policy Planning Group, and Human Resources Group. In '83, two new groups are planned: Government Group and Industrial Marketing Group.

Also, YSW is committed to integrating hands-on consulting capabilities into each group as a separate service area. Towards that end,

YSW in early '83 announced the acquisition of McBer & Company, a Boston-based consulting company specializing in human resources.

There are about 150 full-time, salaried employees at YSW.

Founder and chairman of YSW is Daniel Yankelovich, 58; he is a graduate of Harvard University. President is Florence Skelly, a graduate of Hunter College.

WALKER RESEARCH, INC.
Indianapolis, Indiana

Privately held corporation. Founded in 1964. Research revenues in 1982 were $12.6 million, up 7.8 percent over '81.

This survey research firm, which has 201 full-time employees (80 of whom are salaried), is descended from a local field service organization, Walker Research Service, which was founded in 1939 by Mrs. Tommie Walker Anderson.

Walker is now divided into five divisions. The Operations Division manages a network of branch data collection offices in eight cities, as well as its interactive computer and data processing system. This network provides a variety of interviewing services, including mall intercepts, pre-recruited focus groups, local and national WATS interviewing via CRTs. In total, Walker operates more than 200 phone interviewing stations.

A Special Services Division develops and administers contractual and continuous measurement research programs, and two Account Service Divisions (East and West) are responsible for custom study design, analysis, and interpretive services. Finally, there is a Corporate Services Division.

President and chief executive officer is Frank D. Walker, 48. He is a graduate of DePauw University.

INFORMATION RESOURCES, INC.
Chicago, Illinois

Privately held corporation. Founded in 1977. Revenues in 1982 were $12.3 million, up 109.5 percent over '81.

The main business of this fast-growth company — which in March of '83 offered a block of its common stock for public subscription — is BehaviorScan system, a group of four mini-markets that are set up for controlled store testing. In each market, BehaviorScan can (1) capture product movement data in retail stores via UPC scanners; (2) alternate television advertising over cable TV to groups of pre-selected households; (3) collect purchase data from a panel of about 2,500 households via the use of supermarket point-of-sale UPC scanners; and (4) collect other measures of in-store merchandising/promotions, as relevant. Two new markets were added to the BehaviorScan system in early 1983.

The other major IRI service, called The Marketing Fact Book, makes available access to a data base of purchasing activity on a large number of package goods product classes. Starting in '83, clients will be offered access to this data base on an on-line, interactive basis.

IRI has 224 full-time employees.

President and chief operating officer of IRI is Gian Fulgoni, 35, who has a master's degree from Manchester University in England. Chairman and chief executive officer is John Malec, 38, a graduate of the University of Wisconsin.

LOUIS HARRIS AND ASSOCIATES, INC.
New York, New York

Wholly–owned subsidiary of Gannett Company. Founded in 1956. Research revenues in 1982 were $12.1 million, up 19.8 percent over '81.

About 31 percent of Louis Harris and Associates' volume comes from foreign subsidiaries: Louis Harris International in London and Louis Harris France in Paris. The balance, or $8.4 million, comes from U.S. operations, an increase of 26.5 percent over the comparable number for '81. These domestic volumes include two subsidiaries: The National Center for Telephone Research in New York and Louis Harris and Associates in Washington, D.C. In total, LHA has 130 full-time, salaried employees.

LHA is organized into 13 divisions, each one of which specializes in survey research for different markets, such as public affairs, health care, or banking. LHA also fields multi-client surveys to track corporate, financial, public, and leadership opinions on key issues.

Chairman and chief executive officer of LHA is the company's founder, Louis Harris, 62, the well-known syndicated newspaper columnist (178 newspapers); he is a graduate of the University of North Carolina at Chapel Hill. President and chief operating officer is Humphrey Taylor, 48, who is a graduate of Cambridge University in England.

THE EHRHART-BABIC GROUP
Englewood Cliffs, New Jersey

Privately held corporation. Founded in 1958. Research revenues in 1982 were $11.9 million, up 1.7 percent over '81.

The Ehrhart-Babic Group includes Ehrhart-Babic Associates, Inc., which specializes in custom store audits, controlled store tests and mini-market tests, and National Retail Tracking Index, Inc., which specializes in syndicated observational store stocking checks in various classes of retail trade (e.g., supermarkets, garden, hardware, etc.). During 1982, NRTI's national liquor, wine, and beer panel was supplemented with 2,885 "on-premise" accounts (i.e., restaurants, cocktail lounges, hotels, and bars) in the top 36 markets.

Not included in E-B revenues is Ehrhart-Babic Data Services, Inc., an EDP service bureau.

E-B Group has 111 full-time, salaried employees.

The founders of E-B Group are its current president, Louis J. Babic, Jr., 50, a graduate of Boston University, and the chairman, Thomas A. Ehrhart, 58, a graduate of Pace University.

DATA DEVELOPMENT CORPORATION
New York, New York

Privately held corporation. Founded in 1960. Revenues in 1982 were $11.8 million, up 5.4 percent over '81.

Revenues include all units: Data Development Corporation; Central Location Testing, Inc.; New York Conference Center, Inc.; and The Telephone Centre, Inc., a 40-station interviewing facility which is partially CRT-equipped. All told, there are 120 full-time, salaried employees in four office locations.

In 1983, DDC plans to open a West Coast office and set up a second Conference Center facility in Chicago.

DDC is jointly managed by chairman Jerry Rosenkranz and president Joseph Goldstein. Both are 47 years old and graduates of the City College of New York.

WINONA RESEARCH, INC.
Minneapolis, Minnesota

Privately held corporation. Founded in 1953. Revenues in 1982 were $11.3 million, up 11.9 percent over '81.

This survey research firm, with 150 full-time, salaried employees in three offices (plus two mall operations), includes a WATS-CATI telephone facility with 160 stations, 110 of which are CRT-equipped, in Phoenix (via the acquisition of Research Information Center, Inc. from Greyhound Corporation in March, '82).

President of Winona is Richard McCullough, 39; he is a graduate of the University of Minnesota.

OPINION RESEARCH CORPORATION
Princeton, New Jersey

Wholly owned subsidiary of Arthur D. Little, Inc. Founded in 1938. Revenues in 1982 were $10.2 million, up 24.4 percent over '81.

Opinion Research Corporation, which has 151 full-time, salaried employees, maintains four branch sales/service offices (Chicago, New York, San Francisco, and Washington, D.C.).

In addition to custom, ad hoc studies for agencies of the federal government and industry, ORC does numerous shared-cost surveys periodically, such as the Investment Community Survey; the Public Opinion Index (opinions of target groups, such as business executives, Washington thought leaders, etc.); a Corporate Reputation Survey; The Marketing Index, which tracks trends and issues; Travel Pulse, a study of the travel market; and the Caravan surveys, a pioneer of shared-cost surveys.

President of ORC is Harry W. O'Neill, 54, who holds an MS degree from Pennsylvania State University. Chairman and chief executive officer is Irwin Miller, 54, a vice president of Arthur D. Little. He holds a PhD from Virginia Polytechnic Institute.

HARTE-HANKS MARKETING SERVICES
GROUP — Fair Lawn, New Jersey

The parent is a public company traded on the New York Stock Exchange. The Marketing Services Group was founded in 1975. Revenues in 1982 were $9.6 million, up 2.8 percent over '81.

This research conglomerate, which has been put together by a large, Texas-based publishing firm, Harte-Hanks Communications, grew significantly in 1982 because of two acquisitions: TeleResearch (TV copy testing), Westport, Conn., and TRIM (controlled store tests utilizing UPC scanner data bases), Los Angeles.

The other business units are: RMH Research, Inc. (full service survey firm specializing in communications research), Fair Lawn, New Jersey; National WATS Services (a telephone interviewing facility with 65 stations), also in Fair Lawn; and Urban Data Processing, Inc. (an EDP service bureau specializing in custom processing of Census data for marketing applications), Burlington, Massachusetts.

In total, the company has 125 full-time, salaried employees.

The president of the Marketing Services Group is Richard Hochhauser, 38, the founder of RMH Research, Inc., who also is a vice president of Harte-Hanks Communication. He received his MBA degree from Columbia University.

DECISIONS CENTER, INC.
New York, New York

Privately held corporation. Founded in 1965. Revenues in 1982 were $8.4 million, up 21.7 percent over '81.

Decisions Center, Inc., which has 97 full-time, salaried employees, is divisionalized as follows: Decisions Center, Inc.; Qualitative Decisions Center; DCI International; Murray Hill Center (a focus group facility); and Facts Center, a 63-station WATS telephone interviewing facility. In early '83, DCI opened a branch office in Rochester, New York.

DCI specializes in survey research — concept and product tests, copy research, tracking and trade studies, and large-scale market and strategy studies.

DCI is jointly managed by chairman Bernard Ruderman, 51, who has an MS degree from Pennsylvania State University, and Bernard Levine, 57, who has an MBA from New York University.

McCOLLUM / SPIELMAN / & COMPANY, INC.
Great Neck, New York

Privately held corporation. Founded in 1968. Research revenues in 1982 were $7.1 million, up 16.4 percent over '81.

In October, '82, McCollum/Spielman/& Company acquired Hyatt/Esserman, Inc., and Child Research Services, an operation now called McCollum/Spielman Associates, Inc. Together, these organizations have 69 full-time, salaried employees.

M/S/C's basic business is the pre-testing of TV commercials, print ads, and radio commercials. The main service is called AC-T (for Advertising Control for Television), which uses controlled theater settings in 12 locations around the United States to measure attitude changes in relation to TV commercial exposure.

The new Associates group focuses on survey research and has recently announced two syndicated services.

Chief executive officer at McCollum/Spielman is Harold M. Spielman, 56, who received his BBS degree in sociology from the City University of New York.

STARCH INRA HOOPER, INC.
Mamaroneck, New York

Public corporation traded over the counter. Founded in 1923. Revenues in 1982 were $7 million, up 10.1 percent over '81.

Starch INRA Hooper revenues (which include two wholly owned subsidiaries — The Roper Organization in New York and Daniel Starch Canada Ltd.) in 1982 included $1.4 million from outside the United States. Domestic revenues alone were up 14.9 percent over '81.

This survey firm, best known for print ad and print media audience measures, launched two new syndicated services in '82: FARMS (for Farm Audience Readership Measurement Service) for the agrimarketing industry, and Starch Cable Services (SCS), specializing in TV cable audience measures. (SCS data will be marketed through The Feniger Company, Inc.)

President and chief executive officer is William J. (Jay) Wilson, 46, a graduate of Yale University.

MARKET OPINION RESEARCH
Detroit, Michigan

Privately held corporation. Founded in 1941. Research revenues in 1982 were $6.7 million, up 43.4 percent over '81.

Total Market Opinion Research revenues in 1982 were $7.4 million, of which 89 percent (or $6.7 million) was attributable to five MOR research divisions: Consumer and Industrial, Media, Social, Information Systems, and Political. Much of the increase in revenues in '82 was due to political campaigns; MOR's Political Division is a mainstay with Republican candidates, and in '82 it worked for 33 statewide candidates and 63 Congressional races.

The 260 MOR employees (90 of whom are full-time, salaried) are located in three U.S. offices and one in Toronto, Canada.

During '82, MOR established a new Health Care Marketing Department to assist hospitals and health care agencies in planning and launched a new Geographical Targeting System, which combines census data with client survey data to facilitate small-geography target marketing.

Chairman and chief executive officer of MOR is Frederick P. Currier, 59, who received his MA from the University of Illinois. The president is Robert M. Teeter, 44, who received his MA from Michigan State University.

NATIONAL ANALYSTS
Philadelphia, Pennsylvania

A division of Booz Allen & Hamilton, Inc. Founded in 1943. Revenues in 1982 were $6.6 million, down 1 percent from '81.

This venerable organization specializes in custom survey research and strategic marketing consulting for commercial firms and government agencies. Professional staff specialists focus on (1) financial surveys, (2) telecommunications, (3) the information industry, (4) pharmaceuticals and medical equipment, (5) automotive, (6) packaged goods, and (7) litigation support. There are 73 full-time, salaried employees located in Philadelphia and New York City.

In 1982, NA launched two shared-cost industry studies — one in the field of home information systems and one in transaction volumes of non-credit services for banks.

President of NA is Marshall G. Greenberg, 47; he holds a PhD in mathematical psychology from the University of Michigan.

CUSTOM RESEARCH, INC.
Minneapolis, Minnesota

Privately held corporation. Founded in 1974. Revenues in 1982 were $6.4 million, up 36.2 percent over '81.

This custom survey research firm is now organized into five divisions: Consumer Research; Business-to-Business; Eastern Office (a branch operation located in Union, New Jersey); Corporate Services; and Custom Research Telephone, a central telephone WATS interviewing facility, CRT-equipped, with 40 stations.

There are 75 full-time, salaried employees.

CRI is managed by two partners: Jeffrey L. Pope, 42, who received his MBA from the Kellogg School of Management, Northwestern University; and Judith S. Corson, 40, who is a graduate of the University of Minnesota.

What Would A Top Forty List Look Like?

The cutoff at 30 for 1982's largest U.S. research firms is arbitrary, and it leaves the question, "What would the list look like if the next 10 largest firms were included?"

The exact answer isn't known, but here are seven firms that — most likely — would be included in the expanded listing. In alphabetical order, they are:

AHF Marketing Research, New York. A privately held survey research firm.

Burgoyne, Inc., Cincinnati. Privately held firm specializing in store audits, controlled store tests, distribution checks.

Decision/Making/Information, Santa Ana, California. Privately held custom survey research firm.

Market Research Corporation of America, Stamford, Connecticut. Specialists in mail-diary purchase panels and studies of food consumption in-home. A privately held corporation.

Mediamark Research, Inc., New York. Firm owned by principals and the British firm, Mills & Allen International PLC. Operates a syndicated media/product research service.

Response Analysis, Princeton, New Jersey. Privately held custom survey research firm.

Simmons Market Research Bureau, Inc., New York. Partly owned subsidiary of JWT Group, Inc. Specializes in syndicated service relating media consumption with product usage.

Chapter 11

WORLD'S TOP TEN MARKETING / ADVERTISING RESEARCH ORGANIZATIONS

Each year, after I complete my annual review of the largest U.S. research firms, a key question still goes begging: "How do the largest U.S. firms compare to firms headquartered in other countries?"

So, to answer that, I've taken the first crack at developing a World Top 10 Research Organizations listing, the results of which show in Table 11-1. Six are U.S. companies; four are based in Europe. Five are public companies, and three more are wholly owned subsidiaries of larger, non-research public companies.

This article first appeared in Advertising Age *July 18, 1983.*

Before going on to the company profiles, I should like to thank those people who have, over a period of months, helped me to document nearly 100 non-U.S. research organizations. Their cooperation has been extraordinary, and I should like to acknowledge that. Special thanks to: Ms. Eileen Cole, chief executive, Research International; Wolfgang Ernst, chief executive officer, Infratest Forschung GMBH & Company; Morten M. Lenrow, director, international marketing research, PepsiCo; Jack Brown, chairman, Burke Marketing Services, Inc.; and Ms. Gunilla Broadbent, vice president-director of INRA, at Starch INRA Hooper.

An Introduction to the Top Ten
World Research Companies

Before digesting the revenue estimates for the leading worldwide research companies, I urge you to weigh the following:

- Many of the organizations have total revenues far larger than those listed; my top 10 ranking is based on just that part of their volume attributable to marketing/advertising/public opinion

Table 11-1   World's 10 Largest Marketing/Advertising Research Organizations as of 1982

Organization	Home Country	Approx. Research Revenues, 1982* (Add 000,000)	Number of Countries**
1. A. C. Nielsen Company	USA	$433.1	25
2. IMS International	USA	124.8	34
3. SAMI	USA	85.0	1
4. The Arbitron Ratings Company	USA	80.3	1
5. AGB Research PLC	UK	73.6	20
6. Burke Marketing Services	USA	52.1	2
7. Research International	UK	48.2	29
8. Infratest Forschung G.M.B.H. & Co.	West Germany	32.2	5
9. Market Facts, Inc.	USA	25.4***	1
10. GFK Nurnberg Gesellschaft F Konsum	West Germany	23.9	6
Total		$978.6	

* In many cases total company revenues are significantly larger; see individual company profiles.
** Through subsidiary company or branch office.
*** Does not include Market Facts of Canada, Ltd., with volume of about $2.3 million, in which parent owns about 50 percent.

research. Even though many of these organizations are public, that distinction isn't always as clear-cut as one might like. In any case, the company profiles that follow note the relative importance of research in each organization.

- There are currency conversion values (vis-à-vis the U.S. dollar) to consider, and during the past 18 months these have varied significantly as the U.S. dollar has stiffened. For 1982, I have used for the British pound sterling an average conversion rate of $1.556 to the pound; for the West German DM, I have used 2.4266 to the $1. Still, there is a lot of conversion bounce in these numbers, especially when you consider the number of countries in which some of these organizations do business. (IMS International leads in that respect with operations in 34 countries.)

- Some of these organizations have different fiscal years. I have tried to obtain data for the 12-month period closest to calendar 1982.

- Further, in recent years, many of these organizations have made acquisitions that didn't necessarily result in 100 percent ownership. Exactly how much of that acquisition volume is reflected gets a little hazy at times.

All things considered, I suggest that you consider these 1982 revenues as order of magnitude estimates — but certainly close enough to construct a relative ranking.

It was especially frustrating to try to get a fix on the large Japanese research organizations. One thing, however, seems certain: Those well-known Japanese organizations that specialize in marketing/advertising research — such as Dentsu Research, Chuohchosasha (Central Research Service), the Japan Marketing Research Association, or Video-Audience Research — are not nearly large enough to make a World's Top 10 listing (nor is the largest French firm, SOFRES).

One enigma: The huge Nomura Research Institute in Tokyo, which has revenues in the range of $50 million. Nomura does economic forecasting and social research, much of which is based on secondary source data. But it also does a considerable amount of custom survey research. What percent that is of the total Nomura volume is unknown, but I have no reason to believe that it is large enough to get NRI on the top 10 list.

Company Profiles

A. C. Nielsen Company — USA

Of total revenues for the 12 months ending November 30, 1982, 66.2 percent — or $433.1 million — came from marketing/advertising research activities. ACN set up its first foreign subsidiary in Great Britain in 1939; today it has research operations in 25 countries. Basically these services are store audit programs to develop market size measurements, share of market for brands, and TV audience measurement systems — either on a national or local-market basis. ACN is a public company.

IMS International — USA

Of total revenues for 1982, about 74 percent — or $124.8 million — came from marketing research activities in 34 countries. Basically, this activity consists of market size and brand share measures in fields of interest to the pharmaceutical/medical and health care industry. IMS is a public company.

SAMI — USA

SAMI's basic activity, available in the United States only, is to amalgamate warehouse withdrawal data to produce continuous movement data on thousands of individual package goods items sold through food stores, separately for each of 48 marketing areas. Revenues for

1982 were estimated at $85 million. SAMI is a wholly owned subsidiary of Time, Inc.

The Arbitron Ratings Company — USA

ARC's basic business is local market measurements of radio and TV audiences, mostly via mail diaries and meter-equipped TV sets. They operate only in the United States. Revenues for 1982 were estimated at $80.3 million. ARC is a wholly owned subsidiary of Control Data Corporation.

AGB Research PLC — UK

For the fiscal year ending April 30, 1983, this London-based conglomerate is expected to have total revenues of about $93.4 million, of which about 79 percent — or $73.6 million — will be attributable to research activities in 20 countries. These figures will reflect, for the first time, the approximately $22 million gained through the acquisition of the U.S. research firm, NFO Research, Inc. They would not yet reflect the recent acquisition (in part) of the Survey Research Group in Asia, which will take AGB's activities into six more countries.

Basic AGB activities are (1) consumer panels, (2) TV audience measurement systems (mostly via meter-equipped TV sets), (3) omnibus surveys, and (4) media research. AGB is a public company.

Burke Marketing Services, Inc. — USA

This conglomerate consists of (1) the Test Marketing Group — TV campaign testing and controlled marketing labs; (2) BASES — market modeling; (3) Professional Services — educational seminars; (4) Telcom Research — physiological measures of advertising stimuli; (5) Burke Marketing Research — pre- and post-TV copy testing and custom survey research; and (6) a wholly owned subsidiary, Burke Canada, which accounts for about $1.4 million of the company's revenues. In addition there is Burke International, a joint venture with Infratest, a West German firm also on the top 10 list, in which BMSI owns a 5 percent interest. BMSI is a privately held corporation.

Research International — UK

This organization, which specializes in custom, ad hoc survey research, operates in 29 countries, and there are over 800 full-time employees. Headquarters are in London. In some countries, RI conducts omnibus surveys and diary mail panels.

RI is a wholly owned subsidiary of Unilever Ltd., but less than 40 percent of its work comes from Unilever subsidiaries around the world. RI's total revenues in 1982: $48.2 million.

Infratest Forschung GMBH & Company KG West Germany

This firm, with home offices in Munich, and its four subsidiaries had revenues of $32.2 million in 1982. Infratest operates in five European countries, and there are about 465 employees, about 225 of whom are professionals.

Infratest specializes in ad hoc consumer surveys, advertising and media research, omnibus surveys, and political/public opinion polling. It is a privately held corporation founded in 1947.

Infratest revenues do not include the partial acquisition of Research Services, Ltd., a British survey company, a transaction that took place in early 1983. Also, Infratest and GFK (see below) jointly owned a consumer panel operation, and Infratest sold its share to GFK in early 1983. That transaction is not reflected in either the Infratest or GFK numbers. Also, Infratest owns 5 percent of Burke Marketing Services, another top 10 company.

Market Facts, Inc. — USA

This public company had revenues of $25.4 million in 1982, not including those of a Canadian subsidiary, which is 50 percent owned by the parent; if included, that would add about $2.4 million to MF revenues.

MF's main U.S. activities are: (1) the Consumer Mail Panel, (2) Marketest store audit services, (3) five shopping mall facilities, (4) WATS telephone interviewing, and (5) ad hoc survey research.

GFK Nurnberg Gesellschaft F Konsum und Absatzforschung & V. — West Germany

This organization, which operates in six European countries, had revenues of $23.9 million in 1982. Headquarters are in Nurnberg, and there are about 565 full-time employees.

GFK specializes in a broad range of research activities: ad hoc survey research; advertising research; syndicated surveys; package and product testing; industrial, financial, medical, and agricultural marketing research. GFK, which was founded in 1934, is technically a trade association, and its shares cannot be sold to outsiders.

During 1982, these 10 organizations had, in total, marketing/advertising/public opinion research revenues of about $978.6 million, and the A. C. Nielsen Company alone accounted for 44 percent of that.

Chapter 12

How Much Is Spent on Research in the U.S.?

If there is one question that comes most often to someone who writes about the research industry, this is it. Further, if there is one number that has been guesstimated with reckless abandon in articles in the popular press about the research industry, this is it.

Finally, with a note of exasperation, I tried to put the matter to rest with an explanation of why an exact answer is so difficult — nigh impossible — to calculate. It ran as a column in Advertising Age *June 21, 1982.*

The Question

"How much is spent for research in the United States each year?"

That's the question that comes over my phone most often, and especially just after publication of the top marketing/advertising/public opinion research company listing I prepare for *Advertising Age* each year.

I am getting weary of explaining — and I'm sure frustrated callers are tired of listening to — all the reasons why no one has an exact answer to that question. "But," some callers insist, "can't you make an estimate?" The answer, of course, is "yes" — and that's what I'm finally doing via this article. However, since this magic number is apt to be picked up and bandied around, I urge you to follow the explanation of how it was derived, what's included — and what is not. Laborious this may be, but in the process you'll come to understand how complex the industry is, and why I haven't had a snappy one-line answer for callers through the years.

The Answer

Top Companies

The base from which I depart is the listing of the largest U.S.-owned, for-profit research organizations and their revenues. In total, these 28 organizations had 1981 revenues of $1.25 billion, but only $974.2 million of that came from research activities. Of that, $643.8 million was from research activities within the United States, and since I'm working to approximate how much is spent on marketing/advertising/public opinion research in the United States, that's the prime number: $643.8 million.

As such things go, it's a hard number; many of these top companies are public, and most of the others have been very open about making their revenue figures available to me, along with substantiation from their accounting firms, when requested, through the years. Equally important, these leading firms represent all facets of data collection — survey, syndicated and ad hoc; store audits, syndicated and custom; product movement data gathered via warehouse withdrawal and UPC scanner systems; mall intercepts; copy testing; standing mail panels; media audience measures; diary purchase panels; focus groups; et al. In a word, these companies represent the diverse spectrum of services for which "research money" is budgeted.

CASRO Input

My thanks go to the Council of American Survey Research Organizations (CASRO) for a valuable input. Each year, CASRO member firms supply, on a confidential basis, a statement of their revenues. From the total for 1981, Diane K. Bowers, executive director of CASRO, subtracted out those revenues reported by firms that were on my top listing, and that left $234.6 million in revenues from 80 other CASRO member firms, almost entirely commercial survey research inside the United States. (Included in this group are such prominent firms as Burgoyne, National Family Opinion, Decision/Making/Information, McCollum/Spielman, Houlihan/Parker, and The Gallup Organization, to name just a few.) Add that to the base of $643.8 million, and we have solid documentation of $878.4 million.

However, that still leaves numerous prominent commercial research firms that were either not large enough to be on my top listing or were not members of CASRO in 1981. Here are some conspicuous examples:

Continuous, purchase diary panels: Market Research Corporation of American (MRCA), Para-Test Marketing, and Mail Diary Panel, Inc.

Media audience measures: Statistical Research, Mediamark, Simmons Market Research, and Don Bowdren Associates.

TV/print copy testing: Tele-Research, Gallup & Robinson, Vopan Marketing Research, Telcom Research, Westgate Research, Research Systems Corporation (ARS), Bruzzone Research, and Video Storyboard.

Store measures: Store Audits, Inc.; TRIM; and NABSCAN.

Survey houses: Oxtoby-Smith, Scarborough Research Corporation, Cambridge Reports, Mathematica Policy Research, Marketing Evaluations, RMH Research, Research International (U.S. only), Bee Angell Associates, Lee Slurzberg Research, Goldstein/Krall Marketing Resources, On-Trac Research, Opatow Associates, MPi Marketing Research, and the survey division of ABT Associates.

Based on information they have supplied me or just guesstimates, I think these 32 organizations alone would add about $53 million to our total, taking it up to $931.4 million.

The Hard Part

In addition to the 140 organizations which are included in our running total so far, there are at least 100 other research suppliers, many of which are one-, two-, or three-man shops operative in the United States. As to the revenue this segment of the industry generates, I can only speculate. An average of $250,000 each seems conservative, and if you agree, add $25 million to the total, bringing it up to $956.4 million.

I *do not include* in this category the numerous firms that are basically field service. A few are quite large and some provide full service, ranging from design through analysis. But for the most part, adding in such operations would result in double counting of revenues; that is, their revenues mostly come from subcontract work on projects being conducted by larger firms we've already added in.

Also not included are numerous service firms on the fringe of the research industry, who either specialize in manipulation and/or analysis of marketing data (such as SPAR or Market Science Associates) or analysis of public domain data (such as Majers). Also not included are firms like Frost & Sullivan, Inc., and Business Trends Analysts, Inc., who specialize in reports based on secondary source data.

In-House Research

Next we have to face up to full-scale, in-house research operations, such as those operated by firms like Procter & Gamble, General Mills, General Foods, Quaker Oats, Hill & Knowlton, Ruder & Finn, McGraw-Hill — and advertising agencies, especially Foote, Cone & Belding, Grey, Leo Burnett, Y&R, J. Walter Thompson, and Bates, to name a few. Now estimates get shaky.

Some numbers I pulled together suggest that P&G, Quaker, General Mills and General Foods combined spend in the neighborhood of $25-26 million through their internal research organizations. The problem is that some of that money is spent with outside suppliers, perhaps ones we've already counted in. For instance, say General Foods does its own on-air TV copy testing, but the field work is farmed out to a survey firm, already counted, while design, tabulation, and analysis remain in-house. Double counting again rears its ugly head. The same is true with advertising agencies. Grey Advertising, which has one of the largest agency research departments, for instance, does all its field and tab work through Data Development, one of the 1981 top firms.

So, how much do we tack on for unduplicated in-house research work? I submit that $15 million is a reasonable and conservative number. That brings our running total up to $971.4 million.

The Non-Profits

There are numerous organizations with non-profit corporate charters that specialize in survey research in the United States. According to the Survey Research Laboratory at the University of Illinois, there are 49 such organizations affiliated with and/or operating units of universities alone.

The *Survey Research Newsletter* at the U. of I. did a survey in 1981 that indicates this university group — and there wasn't full reporting — does something in excess of $84 million in survey work a year. Now, if you think that's all academics talking to one another, you're mistaken. Prominent university-affiliated research centers like NORC at the University of Chicago, the Survey Research Laboratory at the University of Illinois, the Survey Research Center at the University of Michigan, Research Triangle, et al., do some of their work for commercial clients. Some are very aggressive in pursuing such business.

For instance, I received a sales letter to potential industrial clients from an outfit called University Resources, which is "affiliated" with The Barney School of Business and Public Administration, University of Hartford (Conn.). It turns out, as a "non-profit," University Resources claims to have done 350 studies (surveys) for commercial clients over the past seven years. It does no work for the faculty at Barney.

I believe that these university-related non-profits should add at least $90 million to our running total, taking it up to $1,061,400,000.

In addition, there are non-university affiliated non-profits that get involved in survey research, such as the Bureau of Social Science Research and the Rand Survey Research Institute. These outfits, like most of the university units, feed off grants from agencies of the federal government and/or foundations who are heavy into social investigations. There are dozens of such organizatons operating in the Washington, D.C., area alone, although their ranks have been thinned by recent cutbacks in federal budgets.

No one has a firm fix on how much this group accounts for, but from my experience I'd say many such organizations subcontract their survey work and/or field to commercial survey research firms or university affiliated non-profits. So even if we had a dollar volume estimate, we'd still be back to the old bugaboo: double counting.

The U.S. Government

Now we arrive at the biggest spender for, and doer of, research of all — agencies of the federal government. No one has an exact fix on this traffic, but Charles Turner and Elizabeth Martin of the National Academy of Sciences have studied the files of the Statistical Policy Division of the OMB and come up with some interesting estimates. Regulations require that agencies of the executive branch of the federal government submit questionnaires and a statement of study plan to the OMB for approval before conducting a survey. One of the reasons is to prevent duplication of effort; another is to prevent overburden on potential respondents.

In any case, this results in an overview of survey traffic — not at all complete — sponsored by government agencies. Looking just at studies where individuals would be interviewed, Turner and Martin found, as of November 1980, that OMB had 202 active files on surveys, and if all went on plan, they would result in 5,245,000 interviews — mail, telephone, and face-to-face. This, they felt, provided an approximation of the annual federally sponsored survey traffic.

Of the 202 studies, 127 were being conducted through non-government suppliers; i.e., commercial firms like Westat or Chilton Research Services, university affiliated survey centers, or non-profit survey firms — expenditures I've already tried to account for. The balance, 75 studies, were to be conducted by federal agencies in-house.

The most conspicuous example of in-house government research is the Demographic Survey Division of the Bureau of the Census, one of the world's largest survey research organizations. (The Bureau's

Field Division has about 400 full-time employees, 3,200 part-time interviewers, and 12 regional offices.)

Most of the surveys done through DSD are funded by agencies of the federal government, but on occasion studies have been done for commercial clients, like trade associations. The DSD had, in fiscal year 1981, "reimbursable revenues" of about $62 million, and in addition did about $4 million worth of work from their own budget. So, from just this one source, let's add $66 million to our running total, bringing it up to $1,127,400,000.

And that still leaves other federal studies done by, as they say in Washington, the "statistical community," for which I have no documentation, especially the National Center for Health Statistics (a unit of HHS — Health and Human Services), which does its own studies and some for outsiders, and the Bureau of Labor Statistics, which does surveys in-house and for other federal agencies. And, added to that, there are thousands of industrial organizations, news media, etc., which do all sorts of surveys now and then, entirely in-house (many of which, in my experience, are methodological monstrosities). No one will ever be able to tote up these expenditures, but let's guess that it's about $75 million, most of which is federal, in-house.

So, the next time someone calls to ask my estimate of how much is spent for research in the United States each year, I'm going to say, "about $1.2 billion — conservatively, without double counting."

Now, if you are with a research organizaton, you can calculate your share of the U.S. market. A. C. Nielsen's share in 1981, for instance, would have been about 14 percent. The 28 largest commercial firms in my 1981 listing, in total, account for about 54 percent.

Chapter 13

TV Copy Testing Flap

Well over $51 million a year is spent on TV copy testing in the U.S., excluding the time charges associated with on-air tests. But the consternation caused by this activity is far out of proportion to the monies spent; this is the most anguished-about segment of the research industry because to many — mostly creatives in advertising agencies — the loose numerical measures of a comercial's probable effectiveness stifle imaginative, breakthrough advertising.

This controversy continues today, and I did my best to put things into perspective in the following article, which appeared in Advertising Age *January 19, 1981. Unfortunately, that presentation dropped out a segment that reflected the viewpoint of some prominent agency creatives. That has been restored, and here's the full story.*

TV Copy Testing Flap: What To Do About It

Then I said, Woe is me! For I am undone . . .

Old Testament

" 'Copy' and 'testing' have become two of the dirtiest words in our vocabulary," pined Richard F. Chay, director of marketing research, S. C. Johnson & Son, in a speech to the American Marketing Association Research Conference in New Orleans in September of 1980. He went on to lament the "open hostility" within the marketing community on this issue, the "abuse" of copy testing techniques, and the "bad image" this flap is imputing to the whole research industry.

And, indeed, no segment of the research industry has been subject to as much public hand-wringing, introspection, and hyperbole as that which specializes in systematic testing of TV copy.

Attendees at the last two American Research Federation conferences and Advertising Age Week have heard numerous articulate and emotional critiques from such heavy hitters as Allen G. Rosenshine, president of BBDO; Shepard Kurnit, chairman of DKG Advertising; Burton Manning, chairman and chief executive officer of J. Walter Thompson, U.S.A.; and Normal L. Muse, at that time executive vice president, creative services, Leo Burnett Company. Their common lament: Creative people "don't want 'report cards' and 'imperfect rules' measuring their work," as Mr. Kurnit puts it.

"All of us, agencies and clients alike, have submitted ourselves to justification by the numbers instead of using those numbers only as an aid to judgment," adds Mr. Rosenshine. "We have had more faith in Mr. Burke, Mr. McCollum, Mr. Spielman, Mr. Mapes, and Mr. Ross than we have had in ourselves. None of this is what excellence in advertising is all about."

To hammer their point, agency speakers often cite case histories — most specifically, the now-famous "Mikey" commercial Doyle Dane Bernbach created for Life cereal and the Pepsi "spirit" commercials created by BBDO — which "wouldn't have been produced and run" had copy testing scores prevailed. And that is one of the rubs. Says an executive at a research firm that specializes in copy testing: "These creative people are much more impressive public speakers than we [researchers] are — and one of the reasons is that they don't have to stick to the facts."

The "Mikey" commercial is a case in point; it was "a very rare instance" when Quaker Oats management put a commercial on air without testing. And, while marketing insiders at Quaker say it resulted in "highly effective advertising," they also point out that during the early period when Life sales gains were so impressive, there were "lots of other marketing factors operative" — such as expanded distribution, deals, and new flavor flankers. Life billings are now at BBDO.

As to the Pepsi "spirit" commercials, there is reason to believe that those highly artistic, "mood" spots have been much more effective in markets where Pepsi is the leader over Coke, where Pepsi's total market presence is greater. In markets where Coke is the leader, the nuts-and-bolts blind taste-test copy has been much more effective in moving Pepsi ahead in its share-of-market race with Coke.

Be all that as it may, today advertising agency leaders — creatives and researchers alike — client marketing people, and some copy research company executives are being especially critical of the whole process through which a creative execution passes before finding itself propelled onto the airwaves with a multi-million dollar budget. And, singled out for special denunciation are the single "magic number" results of on-air recall testing, as exemplified by Burke DAR scores.

Concurrently, advertisers — reacting to the ever increasing cost of TV time — seem to be putting more heat than ever on their agencies and research consultants to find a better way to minimize risk, make copy testing more predictive of sales efficacy.

Improvement Is Possible

There follows a discussion of this controversy, a synthesis of thinking gathered from numerous in-depth discussions with some of the most knowledgeable people in the business. The reader should not expect a panacea to plop out at story's end, but I do believe you'll come to share my conclusion: There is much that can be done now to put matters into perspective and, hence, alleviate much of the friction that exists.

32,500 Commercial Exposures a Year

Let's start with an appreciation of the difficult problem facing an agency "creative." Each day the average American spends about four hours watching TV, and, given the proliferation of 10-second spots, this could mean an exposure to 35 commercial messages an hour, depending upon whether viewing is concentrated in daytime, prime time, late fringe, etc. That makes for about 140 commercial exposures a day, or a potential of 51,100 a year. But, given time off for trips to the toilet and refrigerator, plus some vacation, the estimate of Dave Vadehra, president of Video Storyboard Tests, seems reasonable: 32,500 TV commercial exposures a year. And with heavy viewers, there could be much more.

Our creative friend is told, simply, to do something that will — without running up production costs — cut through that awesome amount of communications traffic (all done by professionals vying for attention), capture a target audience, make a sales message stand out, and persuade people to buy. That task could be coming from a client with a weak, me-too product in a low-interest category — and be communicated secondhand by an account man who isn't too bright. And, oh yeah — we need roughs in a week.

It's easy to understand the "creative's" frustration when, some time later, he is told that, according to the norms of some standardized copy testing service, he has fallen short in a test of rough copy. Go try again.

But I think obviously the other side of that coin is that the demand for such creative talent far exceeds the supply, and then even the best of the creatives can have an off day or have next to no enthusiasm for some particular project that's dumped into their lap.

And that brings us to the Golden Rule.

He Who Has the Gold Rules

This proposition was stated clearly by Jack R. Andrews, director of marketing research at General Foods, at the 1980 ARF Conference: "Few advertisers can afford to invest millions of media dollars and risk important consumer franchises on copy which has only the author's stamp of approval to attest to its effectiveness."

The answer: some quantifiation of sales/communication efficacy — a test — with the client paying for it mostly, either directly or indirectly. And it usually is the client who is specifying the methodology (or service) that is used in measuring rough or finished copy.

Simply, clients tend to agree with Lord William T. Kelvin (1824-1907), the British mathematician and physicist, who said:

> When you can measure what you are speaking of and express it in numbers, you know of what you are discoursing. But when you cannot measure it and express it in numbers, your knowledge is of a very meager and unsatisfactory kind.

An MBA temperament and training can pick up this concept easily. But, as Gerald Lukeman, president of ASI Market Research, Inc., notes: "Writers, producers, and art directors — I'll refer to them as 'creatives' — resist and are afraid of number on all levels."

And there's another rub: The very act of quantifying, of turning to the language of mathematics for expression, goes against the creative temperament. Witness this comment by Dennis Altman, senior vice president/creative director, D'Arcy-MacManus & Masius/de Garmo: "I know this sounds elementary, but you have to remember we're not dealing [referring to clients] with overpowering mentalities here. We're dealing with people who doubt their own ability to rely on anything other than a number." Adds Mr. Lukeman; " 'Researchsers,' in turn, are afraid of/cut off from intuitive processes, suspicious of them, overly rational."

And so the lines are drawn: tests mean quantification, and quantifian creates a communications barrier — at least with some people.

But, equally important, is this thought laid down by JWT's Burt Manning in his ARF speech in 1979:

> Can you blame a copy writer or an art director for being preoccupied with getting a good test score? For trying to beat the system? When creative people know that a commercial has got to score on the test or it doesn't get on the air,

they try to learn the tricks, the devices, the gimmicks that seem to be associated with high scores.

Even more dangerous, I think, is that creative people begin to reject, to pre-censor ideas that do not look promising in the test situation — even if every instinct tells them these ideas might do far better for the product in the real market place. This inhibition of the creative process may be the most costly side effect of all.

Why Blame Copy Testing?

The pique creatives display towards copy testing seems singular and distorted to some research executives. They point out that, from the time a creative has an idea through the time it eventually goes on the air (or is rejected), that idea could have gone through a series of critiques, each of which changed it, or watered it down, a bit.

For instance — first it must clear the creative group head. Perhaps then the agency research department does some in-house testing. Then there could be a review by the agency's creative board. Then the lawyers nitpick the claims, and exactly how they are stated. Production people come up with a production estimate, which may call for some cutting back. The client's ad director makes a tentative approval, and then maybe it goes through a committee of marketing executives at the client's company. Then there's authorization of a budget for rough, or finished production. Maybe then it goes into pre-testing with an outside service and, finally, an on-air post test.

"It seems to me," comments one research executive, "that when those creatives get up in public and lambaste that final step — an on-air recall test — they are copping out. It is their employers, the agency and client, who are curtailing their creative freedom — if in fact anyone is — and that process has taken place before we ever see the reel."

Multi-Faceted Inquiry

The term "copy testing" is used in a singular sense most often, and that contributes to misunderstanding. In fact, the field is diverse, as was neatly summarized by Burt Manning in his 1979 ARF Conference speech:

> This is a manual on copy test... put together by the J. Walter Thompson Research & Planning Department, to serve as a guide to what our research professionls described as "The Leading Methods of TV Copy Testing in Use Today." It describes twenty-four different methods — twenty-four different ways of testing advertising.

I'm told there are a lot more. These are just the twenty-four leading methods. And, interestingly, these twenty-four do not represent subtle or minor variations on a common approach.

There are some radical differences among them — some use one exposure to a test commercial; others use two exposures or more. Some are in-home; others in central locations. Some use recruited audiences and forced exposures; others do not.

Some show commercials in a variable program context, others in a constant context, and still others in no context. Some focus on recall and playback, others on persuasion, others on brand perceptions or diagnostics. Some use verbal measure only; others trace physiological changes — eye movement, voice pitch, brain waves, and on, and on, and on, and on.

This profusion of techniques has several negative implications. For one, some techniques were developed to focus on just one aspect of the TV commercial communication prowess at one stage of the developmental process — and are, in fact, used by clients eager to save money to serve a broader purpose — misused and abused.

Another implication is that copy testing is a competitive business, and one service may well try to make hay by knocking the competitor's methodological weakness; this negative selling seeps through to creatives who then conclude "a pox on all your houses." And, finally, profusion leads to a communications barrier, as articulated by Mr. Lukeman: "There are very few meaningful, ongoing training programs designed to familiarize writers with copy testing procedures. Meaningful familiarity with these procedures would eliminate 50 percent of the difficulties. We tend to be less resistant to, and less suspicious of, things we understand."

Another dimension of copy testing activity comes from estimates developed in a recent confidential study: over 9,800 commercial tests (not commercials tested; any one could go through two or more tests) done in the U.S. each year at a cost of about $34 million. On-air recall testing alone, it is estimated, has an annual volume of $12 million.

Fighting the Curve

One of the attractions of large standardized testing procedures — such as ASI, Burke, McCollum/Spielman, Mapes and Ross, ARS, The Sherman Group, Gallup & Robinson, et al. — is that since they have tested so many commercials in basically the same way, they have developed "norms" — data banks of scores from thousands of commercials, against which a new commerical score can be compared.

That helps put the new commercial into perspective: "How does, for instance, a new HBA product commercial compare to those other HBA efforts that have gone before?" These scores come to constitute a statistical field of their own, and, as with any such large base of observations, you would expect to find a normal distribution curve.

This distribution, which is the same process a student at school is subject to in a course where the teacher "grades on the curve," is a relative measure and, by its very nature, conductive to friction; by definition, half the commercials tested will be below the norm or average. And that leads to a situation where a specific creative, or his advertising agency, scores "below average" — an ego-bending notion that obviously gets creative hackles up.

Are some clients so arbitrary that they stop production of a commercial that is below average? Yes, indeed — it's a policy in some companies, but not all. According to Donald E. Siebert, vice-president in charge of DAR activities at Burke Marketing Research, "It does happen, of course — but not as much as people think; the real cutoff is the bottom quartile."

Another function of the curve is that, by definition, most commericals are clustered in a central "average" field; very, very few will get extremely high scores.

Ten Ways to Improve the Situation

Earlier in this discourse, I alluded to the fact that much could be done right now to alleviate much of the friction that exists between creatives and the copy testing syndrome — starting with trying to put the whole flap into perspective. Accordingly, I pass on 10 specific suggestions which, collectively, represent the best advice of some of the most knowledgeable people immersed in the problem. Take them to heart, and you too might get better creative from your agency.

1. Appreciate the difficult problem a "creative" faces — cutting through, impacting is much easier said than done.

2. Don't expect the discipline of copy testing to go away. It's wise to heed this observation of the late Dr. Oscar Morgenstern, the famous econometrician: "Wherever mathematics has entered, it has never again been pushed out by other developments. The mathematization of an area of human endeavor is not a passing fad; it is a prime mover of scientific and technological progress." Change, improve — yes; go away, no.

3. Involve the creative in the research process; the more he/she feels part of it and understands what is being measured and why, the more he/she is apt to learn from the process rather than resent it, which is counter-productive. (For new people coming

into the business, I recommend the AAAA-sponsored booklet, "What Every Young Account Representative Should Know About Creative Research," by Daniel M. Lissance and Leland E. Ott.)

4. Work with the agency as a partner. "I've been giving presentations for 20 years, and my estimate is that 80 percent of the time the agency and advertiser are in an adversarial relationship," notes Mr. Lukeman. "This is really mind-boggling when one thinks about it."

5. Spend the money to do it right. "When you compare the cost of information to broadcasting costs, it is obviously self-defeating to skimp on copy testing," says Michael von Gonten, late of Research Systems Corporation, and now with the BASES division of Burke. The corollary says, "Don't take the results from one test, which was designed to measure just one aspect of the communications process, and expect it to serve as a substitute for another service, which was designed to measure others."

6. A clear-cut statement of copy strategy, up front, saves much anguish later. Oftenthe copywriter is not given explicit direction, and later a piece of copy written to accomplish one objective is tested and evaluated according to how well it did something else.

7. Always remember, when copy testing, the abominations — blithefully labeled "creative" — that flood into the system and, appropriately, should get screened out by testing. "What I'd love to do," says the president of one copy testing service, "is follow one of these creative spokesmen at ARF and show a reel of commercials that got low scores. Nothing would make the point better; most of the stuff that gets shot down is awful — in fact, some of the stuff that gets on the air is awful."

8. Beware the middleman. Almost every copy testing executive I talked to underscored the deadening effect of middlemen — functionaries who get between copy testing experts and creatives. "The system keeps us apart," says one, "and the creatives are never invited to our presentations. If they could hear what we say first-hand, I don't think there would be nearly as much antagonism."

9. Copy testing has an adverse effect on an agency's bottom line. The more testing, the more rejections of copy executions, the more meetings, and the more creative staff manhours needed to handle the business — the higher the cost of doing business. Agencies are in business to make money when all's said and done,

and it's natural that they would have an aversion to anything that makes that harder.

10. And, finally, always ask: "Am I part of the problem?" — a copy testing executive who knows little about the process of advertising or marketing; the copywriter who indiscriminately scoffs at copy testing over lunch at Crist Cellas but who — for the life of him — couldn't explain how the various services work; or the client who gets spooked at the slightest negative along the creative process way.

In a word, the whole copy development procedure is fraught with communications breakdowns/barriers, many of which are man-made. Intelligent men can get rid of many of them.

Copy Testing Techniques

Day-After Recall

The history of day-after recall measures of a commercial's ability to cut through and etch memorability in a natural on-air viewing situation — the roots of Burke's DAR — traces back to Princeton, New Jersey in the late 1940s. Dr. George Gallup, Sr., then active in Gallup & Robinson, Inc., became intrigued with the problem of measuring commercial effectiveness, which in those days was within a context of 60 seconds, no clutter, and sole-sponsor shows. He started by acquiring the rights to R&D done by a Commander Thompson in conjunction with the training of Navy pilots in WW II.

G&R experimentation led to a 24-hour (day-after) recall with aided recall to the product class level. (Later, with proliferation of set ownership and commercials, aid was extended to the brand name level.) Numerous advertisers were interested in his work, recalls Earnest A. Rockey, now president of G&R, but a young assistant to Dr. Gallup in those days. A syndicated service was started by G&R in 1950, and the concept was "Impact."

A bit later, Compton Advertising started work on a similar system called CSMI (for Compton Sales Message Index). "We started with the forgetting curve work of Ebbinghaus [1886]," recalls Howard Kuhn, now retired, but manager of research at Compton in those days. "We tested the recall on commercials 12, 24, 48, and 72 hours after exposure and finally settled on 24 hours — an arbitrary decision — where there was still enough recognition of copy ideas to evaluate impact."

An extensive amount of testing was done, "all at the initiative and expense of Compton," says Mr. Kuhn "and we examined all the variables — type of show, differences from city to city, daytime/night time, internal spots versus those at the beginning and end of a show, and so on." Out of all this, there were two major conclusions: (1) "artificial exposure of a commercial" in a controlled setting was "no good"; it led to artificially high recall; and (2) of all the variables tested, "the key measure was the 'staying power' of the commercial message over and beyond any advertising history the brand had." The CSMI service was finalized in 1952.

Development of CSMI techniques was followed closely by Procter & Gamble, which was doing some R&D of its own, including double bind tests. The result was what at P&G were then called "In-the-Market Studies," and the field work was handled through a then-small research company in Cincinnati called Burke. "We fell heir to business," recalls Donald L. Miller, past president [and owner] of the company that today is known as Burke Marketing Services, Inc., "because we had the only field force capable of doing it [i.e., executing the P&G questionnaire with numerous open-end questions]. The first DAR we did for P&G was in Bloomington, Indiana, in 1952 on the 'Loretta Young Show' — and it was all door-to-door interviewing in those days."

When P&G was sold on the technique, all their advertising agencies were urged to use it, and the field work went through Burke. But tabulation and analysis remained within P&G's MRD as it does to this day.

"P&G was very secretive about the technique," says Mr. Miller, "and they guarded it like one of their product formulations; they felt they had a considerable advantage over the competition." Consequently, for several years, all Burke's work was for P&G agencies. Slowly, but surely, P&G alumni at other companies wanted the same, and this led to Burke's making DAR measures available to other companies in the early 1960s.

No doubt, the mystique of a secret project for P&G had much to do with the ultimate acceptance of Burke's DAR service.

As to P&G, one of their few public statements on the subject appeared in the *Journal of Advertisng Research* in February of 1972; John D. Henry, manager of P&G's MRD then and now, wrote this:

> We do on-air testing, and we talk to consumers following exposure without ever having recruited them to look at the advertising. In our judgment, this is the way one should look at the advertising. In our judgment, this is the way one should measure communication: as it has to take place in the real world — fighting for attention and memory and reaction against all the advertising that competes for a share of the consumer's mind. That's doing it the hard way, I guess, but that's how it is in the real world as we see it.

"Two agencies — Compton and DFS — promoted the technique," notes Mr. Miller, now retired, "but mostly agencies have bad-mouthed it since the beginning."

In addition to Burke, there are five other research companies now providing recall measures, including ASI's Recall Plus, Gallup & Robinson, and Mapes and Ross, Inc. — both Charles F. Mapes, Jr., and Harold L. Ross., Jr, are former employees of G&R. An estimated $12 million is spent each year on such work, and some large package goods manufacturers do their own recall studies in-house.

This one final observation from Sanford L. Cooper, past president of Burke Marketing Research: "DAR only tells you about 20 percent of what you want to know about a commercial — but that's a very important 20 percent.

Persuasion Testing

The concept of measuring simulated sales response to a commercial exposed to a target audience in a controlled, off-air setting to determine sales efficacy traces back to Horace S. Schwerin who, in 1946, founded Schwerin Research Corporation along with colleagues Henry H. Newell and Leonard Kudisch.

Schwerin, who in the beginning was doing delayed recall studies, too, came to believe "the obvious truth that a claim can be well remembered but completely unimportant to the prospective buyer of the product — the solution the marketer offers is addressed to the wrong need," as he puts it in his book, *Persuasion in Marketing*, published in January 1981. "Pretesting in a central location using a motivated, considered-purchase measure seemed to offer the most likely means of predicting campaign testing." Thus, the emphasis was on shifts in attitude, or predisposition to buy a product, within a well-defined target group.

The impact of Schwerin and his early work in this direction is evidenced by the number of former SRC employees who are now prominent in the TV copy testing industry: Gerald Lukeman, president of ASI Market Research, Inc.; Harold M. Spielman and Donald H. McCollum, co-presidents of McCollum/Spielman & Company, Inc.; Martin Weinberger, executive vice president of Oxtoby-Smith, Inc.; and Margaret H. Blair, president of ARS-Research Systems Corporation. (Ms. Blair and her partner, Reginald B. Collier, purchased SRC from Mr. Schwerin in 1968. Mr. Schwerin is currently vice president in charge of market planning, Canned Foods Division, Campbell Soup Company.)

From the beginning, Mr. Schwerin decided to sell to advertisers — not advertising agencies. The reason: "Agencies weren't good longterm prospects; as soon as they got a bad score, they would want to fire you. Besides, in those days, most agencies were doing their own copy testing, and naturally they wanted clients to believe their way was best. One large advertiser who had seven agencies asked them to rate all the copy testing services. Six rated their own first and SRC as second. Only one rated SRC first."

In *Persuasion in Marketing*, Mr. Schwerin notes that in those days, "The majority of major advertisers were retaining either SRC or ASI for the purpose [pre-testing of commercials] and that the technique was even more savagely attacked than is Burke recall today was merely symptomatic of the fact. It might indeed be said that, to vary the old fable, agencies have found that one King Stork has been substituted for another."

"You see," Mr. Schwerin told me recently, "we were attacking the basic legend — that an ad agency is like a doctor; you take his pills. We said, 'An agency is a creative source.'"

Particularly strong supporters of Mr. Schwerin and his attempts to measure persuasion were Charles Beardsley, president of Miles Laboratories; Irving and Neison Harris of Toni; and Leonard Lavin, president of Alberto-Culver. Mr. Lavin, especially, was quite outspoken about advertising — and agencies. "Agency review boards cause more damage than any other single group of people in the advertising process, except perhaps for clients," he is quoted as saying. Other early supporters: General Mills and AT&T Long Lines, according to Mr. Schwerin.

Physiological Testing

The concept of physiological measures, as applied to TV copy testing, is that consumers have emotional responses — basically subliminal — to stimuli (such as elements which make up a commercial) which cannot be verbalized or, if they were verbalized, might be misleading. But these responses can be measured through controlled studies of bodily functions.

This leads to the development of sophisticated equipment that records, as the respondent is being exposed to an advertising message, such bodily fluctuations as eye pupil dilation, brain wave activity, and changes in voice pitch, to mention the most prominent.

This physiological school of inquiry is currently enjoying a boomlet for three reasons: (1) technical improvement in the recording equipment, making it lighter, more portable, and more accurate — coupled with computer analysis; (2) increasing emphasis on "emotional" commercials where, in lieu of a flat-out, reason-to-buy copy point, the consumer is exposed to a series of non-verbal gratification promises which associate with the product inferentially; and (3) increased heat from advertisers to find some sort of predictive "breakthrough" in communications research.

Further, it represents the desire to take what is both a nebulous and ephemeral happening (i.e., exposure to a commercial) and subject it to the dictum of August Comte, the French mathematician-philosopher (1798-1857): "There is no inquiry which is not finally reducible to a question of numbers." Or, as Lee S. Weinblatt, president of Telcom Research, Inc., a firm specializing in eye movement analysis, puts it: "We're called upon to distinguish between 'entertainment' and 'communication.'" Glen A. Brickman, president of Vopan Marketing Research, the leading firm in voice pitch analysis, adds this: "What we're after is the degree of feeling behind a consumer's verbal expression of attitude. Is the consumer committed, or paying lip service?"

Interest in physiological reactions goes way back. According to one expert, jade dealers of yore would shield their eyes when examining stones for purchase; they knew their pupils would react when they viewed a particularly attractive one, a tip-off for the seller to ask a higher price. And poker players wear eye shades for the same reason — and so on.

Clinical psychologists in academe have worked with physiological measures for years, and it was one such — a Dr. R. Hess from the University of Chicago — who worked with Marion Harper, the flamboyant head of McCann-Erickson (and Marplan) in the early 1960s, to measure eyeball movement of respondents as they scanned ads. Behind Harper's auspices, experimentation in physiological measures became fashionable in advertising circles — and used by such heavy weights as Coca-Cola, Buick, and Miles Laboratories.

The Marplan group specializing in this work broke up in the late 1970s, and two alumni now head firms prominent in eye movement research and analysis: Lee Weinblatt of Telcom Research, Inc., and Elliot Young of Perception Research Services, Inc.

The role of brain wave analysis is best described by these excerpts from literature published by Psychophysiological Research Management Company, which is headed by William Harvey: "Recent advances in psychobiology — the study of brain and behavior — have allowed researchers to apply techniques developed for medical and psycho-physiological research to the field of advertising... The evoked potential is a brain wave test in which a computer teases out the amplitude with which a person's brain registers a piece of information. The evoked potential is so fine a measure of attention that mere milliseconds in the response a person makes to a word or image makes the difference between high or low attention value... The right/left hemisphere ratio score tells which half of a person's brain is reacting. If the right dominates, the person's brain is reacting to a picture and/or emotions; if the left dominates, it is reacting to words and/or logical reasoning."

Are advertising agencies receptive to this sort of probing? "It's a given that they'll [creatives] be negative at first; it really depends on how you present yourself," says Mr. Brinkman. Mr. Weinblatt is more outspoken: "For an industry that is supposed to be informing and changing buying habits, they [the agencies] are the most resistant when it comes to learning new things, changing their own habits." Add this observation of John E. O'Toole, president of Foote, Cone & Belding, re the whole physiological scene: "The entrails of sheep are just as valid."

Most physiological testing is specified — and paid for — by advertisers.

Top Creatives — What They Say

I sought out three prominent, highly successful "creatives" to make sure their point of view could be included in the context of this article. They are: David J. Scott, executive vice president, Ogilvy & Mather, Inc.; Lois G. Ernst, president, Advertising to Women, Inc.; and John E. O'Toole, president, Foote, Cone & Belding.

All three agree, albeit reluctantly, to three things:

1. The current flood of public denunciation of copy testing stems in large part from frustration; the "creatives" perceive that now, more than ever, the "numbers people" are winning the game. "It's getting worse," laments Mr. Scott. "The numbers bind is worse today," adds Ms. Ernst.

2. Most of the bad-mouthing comes from the less successful copy writers, not from the top-flight people. As Ms. Ernst points out, "About 90 percent of the time it's the weak copywriters who get the bad scores — but then there's the 10 percent when it 's something brilliant — visionary — that scores low; that's the problem."

3. Some copy writers job hunt on the basis of being able to manipulate the system — i.e., produce copy that scores well. "It's a minority," observes Mr. O'Toole, "and they don't exactly say it flat out — but as they show their reels and Burke scores, the inference is clear. It would be a disservice to our clients if we hired on that basis."

(Jacking up an awareness score is, obviously, an open part of creative trade talk: "There isn't a copywriter worth a damn," says Mr. O'Toole, "who doesn't know how to get a good Burke." Advises Ms. Ernst: "Putting something irritating up front always gets a higher score." And, adds Mr. Scott, who is more articulate that the whole copy research industry combined, "I just put a gorilla in a jock strap when I want a good Burke.")

"I don't fight copy testing," says Ms. Ernst, "and I think any copy writer who does is not wise; after all, you can't expect an advertiser to spend money without some assurance. It's useful — if used correctly." And that's the rub — it's so often misused in her opinion. "Take the way focus groups are used to evaluate concepts and commercials — they [the client] say they just want to 'get a feel, an impression,' and then just one person makes a negative remark and an excellent idea can get killed; there's too much emphasis on 'quick and dirty' research that doesn't quantify anything." Ideally, concludes Ms. Ernst, "The agency and client should truly be business partners — work together to make a good judgment — with 49 percent of the decision based on test scores and 51 percent based on experience and professional judgment."

"It's a savage business," says Mr. Scott, "but all creative people want is a 'fair shot.' The commercial is everything; consumers buy the commercial, not the product — and the commercial should create a rehearsal for purchase. But not enough money is spent up front in putting together the selling equation. Then we need to send through more torpedoes (i.e., copy executions), the more the better, to get home runs instead of singles."

"What is frustrating," adds Mr. O'Toole, "is that creatives do not reject copy testing for the usual reasons, the ones stated so often, such as resistance to a 'report card.' The main reason is that they can't be convinced logically that the tests predict probable effectiveness on-air; results are just too inconsistent — sometimes it seems as if it's just a matter of luck. And," he adds emphatically, "to turn down a commercial on the basis of low recall score is a repudiation of everything that has gone before. It's an irrational act — madness."

And a final observation, again from Mr. O'Toole: "Both sides have dug in to the point where they don't listen to one another any more."

Chapter 14

The Research Function in Top U.S. Advertising Agencies

Given that research has been inherent in the advertising agency business since almost day one — and as far back as 1929 Young & Rubicam set up what is believed to be the first formal agency research department (headed by a young statistical professor from Indiana, George H. Gallup, Sr.) — you'd expect that today the large agencies would be very much aware of what one another was doing in the research field.

To my surprise, I found this was not so. This revelation came from talking with the people who headed some of the largest agency research departments in the summer of 1982. While most could talk knowingly about one or two competitors, they were at a loss to describe knowingly what was going on generally.

So, when the following round-up article appeared in Advertising Age *October 18, 1982, it contained what was to many surprising revelations, especially in how the emphasis on research (in terms of staffing, expenditures) differed from one major agency to another.*

I have since learned that now, when young people want to job jump from one agency's research operation to another, they cite material from this article to explain their reasons why.

An Overview

In 1879 N.W. Ayer & Son, the famous advertising agency then based in Philadelphia, was soliciting a new account, Nichols-Shepard Co., a manufacturer of agricultural machinery. Ayer prepared a media schedule that was challenged by the would-be client, according to L. C. Lockley, writing in *The Journal of Marketing* (April, 1950). Substantiation came from an Ayer survey of state officials and publishers throughout the country asking for information on grain production and media circulation by counties. The client was impressed, and Ayer got the account.

In that respect, at least, things haven't changed much over the past 103 years. When agencies pitch new business, the presentation is often larded with information about the would-be client's marketing problems. But now a large, in-house staff of professional researchers is usually available to gin up the sales ammunition. ("We usually end up setting the tone for the whole presentation," says one agency research director, "because we're the one who have the facts.")

Young & Rubicam claims to have started the first formal agency research department in 1929, the year that a famous statistical professor from Indiana, Dr. George H. Gallup, Sr., came to New York City at the behest of Ray Rubicam to start a department.

Y&R's claim may be disputed, but there is no doubt that research — advertising, media, and market — has been an integral part of U.S. advertising agencies' service capabilities for a long, long time. The roots are deep.

But, currently, there may well be what one research director termed "an identity crisis," with some agency research department heads, at least, casting about for new and more important ways to serve their constituencies and a clear-cut "mission." This has been induced, in part, by the growing sophistication of their clients' research departments; clients aren't so dependent on agency research backup as they once were. Put another way, it's gotten much more difficult to snow a client research-wise.

Also, one of the most sensitive areas of research, testing of TV copy and advertising effectiveness in general, has been under heavy attack — and it is implied that an agency's research staff should somehow alleviate the problem, which continues to fester.

In any case, advertising agencies today fund a sizable segment of the U.S. research industry. For instance, the 25 largest agencies (in terms of gross income derived from U.S. operations alone in 1981) now employ 1,550 people working directly in research of whom 1,162 are considered professionals — according to a unique census recently conducted for this article. And this count does not include about 200 other employees who work in agency libraries or "information centers" as backup to the research staffs or hordes of part-time employees and consultants. So, looking at just the 25 largest U.S. agencies, they collectively employ 5.4 professional researchers per $10 million of gross income.

But the disparity among the 24 largest U.S. agencies in terms of their apparent emphasis on the research function is surprisingly high, as the analysis in Table 14-1 shows. The number of research professionals employed per $10 million in income ranges from a high of 9 (Needham, Harper & Steers) to a low of 2.6 (Ogilvy & Mather). This same variance shows in the percentage of the total agency's payroll going to research staffers. In U.S. agencies with $13.5 million in gross

**Table 14-1   How 24 Large U.S. Advertising Agencies Rank:
The Number of Research Professionals Employed
Per $10 Million in Gross Income (U.S. Only)***

		Total Number Professionals Employed	Number of Professionals Per $10 Million Income
1.	Needham, Harper & Steers	53	9.0
2.	BBDO	106	8.3
3.	Leo Burnett	100	8.1
4.	Foote, Cone & Belding	79	6.8
5.	Ted Bates — New York	40	6.5
6.	D'Arcy-MacManus & Masius	47	6.4
7.	Young & Rubicam (excl. Marsteller)	106	6.1
8.	Kenyon & Eckhardt	29	6.0
9.	Dancer-Fitzgerald Sample	41	5.4
10.	Cunningham & Walsh	20	5.4
11.	Doyle Dane Bernbach	62	5.4
12.	J. Walter Thompson USA	83	5.4
13.	SSCB — New York	22	5.3
14.	Benton & Bowles	43	5.3
15.	Marschalk Campbell-Ewald	34	5.2
16.	N. W. Ayer	35	5.1
17.	Grey Advertising	47	5.0
18.	Ketchum Communications	17	4.4
19.	McCann-Erickson	30	4.0
20.	Bozell & Jacobs	23	3.7
21.	Marsteller Inc.	16	3.2
22.	Wells, Rich, Greene	20	3.1
23.	Subsidiary companies of Ted Bates & Co., combined — most notably Wm. Esty	39	2.9
24.	Ogilvy & Mather	41	2.6

* This analysis was based on gross agency income, U.S. only, for the year 1981, as reported in the *Advertising Age*, 1982 Edition, "U.S. Agency Income Profiles." The research staff counts were furnished directly to the author. The analysis is complicated by the number of subsidiaries included in some agency totals, and for the 10 largest agencies, this is explained in the profile. When possible, data on some of the largest subsidiary agencies are shown separately. Compton Advertising, which is one of the 25 largest agencies, would not contribute to the summary.

income or more, the mean is close to 4 percent. But the range is from a high of over 7 percent in one agency to a low of less than 1 percent in another. Such a swing can't be explained away by caliber of staffs or salary levels; it simply demonstrates that some agencies place much more emphasis on the research function, and that aspect of service to clients, than others. I might add, that is also true when it comes to expenditures for research R&D, agency support for broad-based orig-inal research that might prove useful to all clients, as well as the advertising community in general.

Beyond various dimensions of size, it turns out that there are other significant differences among major agency research opera-tions. For instance, in some, almost all the top research personnel are female; in others, the opposite is true. In some agencies, there is a titular head of research operations — a prominent front man (or woman) — who has a grandiose title (but not necessarily much line authority); in other agency setups, the research staffs scattered around in branch offices and subsidiaries are, for all practical pur-poses, autonomous. Some agencies have through the years built up internal data collection capabilities — focus-group facilities, WATS phone centers, or mall locations for central interviewing — while others farm out almost all their work. Some agency research depart-ments stress their role in helping to make good, effective advertising; in others, the emphasis is on the planning of marketing strategy. Some agencies have a monolithic, highly structured point of view toward some research methodologies (for instance, one TV copy testing service versus another); in other agencies that does not exist, or so I've been told by research suppliers who work almost entirely with agencies.

In a word, these agency research organizations are not nearly as homogeneous as one might expect, and the differences transcend those that might be expected because of their particular client base. This, I think, will become very evident as the reader progresses through the profiles of the 10 largest U.S. agency research opera-tions, which appear later in this article.

Agencies, Clients Differ

Not surprisingly, agencies — it seems — tend to see the research services they offer to clients as being well received and valuable, but the client's evaluation is not necessarily as rosy. The best documenta-tion I can find of this comes from an *Advertising Age* Sounding Board survey conducted in January, 1979. These data are based on a survey of over 100 marketing and advertising executives on the client side and top agency executives. The results, as they pertain to the impor-tance of research at agencies, are shown in Table 14-2.

These data, while certainly not definitive, do suggest that adver-tising research is the important thing from the client's point of view. The importance of marketing research, relatively, is much less.

But, in terms of evaluating how agencies deliver on client expec-tations, Tables 14-3 and 14-4 show the degree to which a gap exists (at least in 1979).

Table 14-2 How Clients Feel About the Importance of Agency Services

	Absolutely Necessary (%)	Very Important (%)	Of Less Import- ance (%)	Not Very Important (%)	NA (%)
Advertising research	23	50	23	2	2
Marketing research	4	25	54	10	7
Marketing strategy and plans	6	52	35	2	5

So, from the agency point of view, 23 percent say clients are "extremely satisfied" with agency contributions to advertising research, and none say clients are "unsatisfied." The client point of view, in sharp contrast, shows that only 4 percent say they are "extremely satisfied," and 23 percent are "unsatisfied."

This is not to say that down deep top executives of major agencies do not recognize this gap and feel it is important enough to take action. It is interesting to note that since 1979, two major agencies — Young & Rubicam and Ted Bates — have brought in new top research management, to a large extent replaced almost all their research professionals, greatly expanded their research staffs, and started to invest in R&D.

Beyond these conspicuous cases, there appears to be a considerable amount of shuffling around at major agencies in response to current criticism and pressure. Here are some examples:

- Leo Burnett, as part of a reorganization in mid-1980, moved senior research staff members physically into the creative department to promote day-to-day cooperation and rapport. The results have been very positive, says Calvin W. Gage, Burnett's research director. At Y&R, New York, senior researchers have been assigned to creative group heads, although they haven't physically moved their offices.

- Almost all major agencies now stress ongoing "life style" research, a continuous monitoring of societal changes and shifts

Table 14-3 How Satisfied Agencies Believe Their Clients Are With Agency's Performance

	Extremely Satisfied (%)	Satisfied (%)	Unsatis- fied (%)	Don't Use/Offer (%)	NA (%)
Advertising research	23	69	—	—	8
Marketing research	11	66	—	9	14
Marketing strategy and plans	46	51	—	—	3

**Table 14-4   Client Degree of Satisfaction with Their Agency's
Performance**

	Extremely Satisfied (%)	Satisfied (%)	Unsatisfied (%)	Don't Use (%)	NA (%)
Advertising research	4	54	23	8	11
Marketing research	4	35	13	33	15
Marketing strategy and plans	4	60	13	15	8

in attitudes and purchasing behavior, to give their agency and
clients an early warning system on the future — and, presumably,
to give their research departments a futuristic image. One
researcher, who headed a large agency research department in
New York, sees this emphasis on "macro" research — the "big
picture" — as a way to compensate for the fact that clients are
less and less interested in workaday research from their agencies.
And it's good publicity for the agency, too.

- Many of the large agencies are starting to play up "strategic
planning" in both job titles and operative roles. Presumably
this stance — in part semantic manipulation — adds prestige and
luster, beyond what can be obtained via research alone. (This has
been going on in British agencies for some time. I've been told
that it's tough to find a "researcher" in London agencies these
days; the operative description now is "strategic planner.")

- A growing response to criticisms about traditional copy testing is
evident too. One conspicuous illustration is the funding by Foote,
Cone & Belding of a new, on-air TV commercial testing procedure they felt was most suitable for evaluating the impact of
highly emotional copy treatments, with emphasis on nonverbal
communications, rather than the traditional day-after-recall
techniques, which tend to place most emphasis on a respondent's
ability to feed back (i.e., verbalize) key copy points, or a selling
proposition. In an unprecedented move, FC&B executives put
together a road show and made public presentations of the findings to meetings of advertising executives in several major cities.

- Another illustration is the PACT report, supported by a group of
20 or so major agencies, which attempts to publicize a standard
point of view re TV copy testing procedures, which — ideally —
would influence all agencies and their clients, settle some dust,
etc.

Quite independent of how large agencies shift and mold their
research operations in the future to position them in a changing

climate, the fact remains that they have been, and continue to be, a large and important part of the U.S. research industry. A profile of each of the 10 largest agency research operations follows, and the scope of their operations speaks for itself.

Agency Research Profiles

YOUNG & RUBICAM — New York

Y&R, the largest agency in terms of U.S. gross income ($222.8 million in 1981), is — along with a group of branch offices and wholly owned subsidiaries, including Marsteller, Inc. — the largest employer of research personnel: a total of 136, of whom 122 are professionals. (This number does not include a library staff, business managers, and clerical support staff; under the Y&R organization in New York, secretaries are on another budget.)

This works out to an average of 5.5 professionals per $10 million in gross income. However, for Y&R properties excluding Marsteller, it is 6.1; for Marsteller alone, it is 3.2.

It wasn't always this way. Since Joseph T. Plummer came from Leo Burnett Company to be executive vice president/director of research, at Y&R USA in 1979, the Y&R research staff has nearly tripled in size. Also, there has been a far greater investment in basic R&D plus a reorganization that emphasizes close working relationships with creatives. (A researcher is assigned personally to each senior creative chief.) The research emphasis, according to an agency statement, has shifted from "How did we do?" to "Are we touching the consumer?"

"This shift from 'counting noses' after the fact to 'sticking our necks out' up-front has had an important impact on creative strategy, creative development and agency new business efforts," according to a Y&R spokesman.

The Y&R research department was founded by George H. Gallup, Sr., in 1929, and that — says Y&R — makes it the oldest agency research group in the United States. Today, the organization includes the traditional account research groups (seven) assigned to clients. This staff is headed by John Eighmey.

In addition, there is a Consumer Research Services group, under the direction of Max Bonfeld, which works in the areas of copy testing, survey design, modeling and computer application, and consumer values/life style research.

Also, a group called Creative Research Services, headed by Susan Gianinno, works on creative problems and manages the Discussion Lab, an in-house focus-group facility.

Paul Murphy is director of research for all Y&R specialty companies (excluding Marsteller, Inc., whose research head is John H. Morris), who can turn to Y&R USA staff for "additional horsepower" on research projects, as required.

Mr. Plummer, 41, in addition to being an executive vice president of Y&R USA, is a member of the Board of Directors. He received his PhD in communications from Ohio State University.

BBDO — New York

While ranking fifth among U.S. agencies in gross income ($127.9 million in 1981), BBDO ranks first in emphasis on research in many respects. The parent plus a passel of subsidiaries, including the recently acquired Tracy-Locke, employ 143 people in research, 106 of whom are professionals. (These numbers do not include seven employees in the Information Resource Center, which is touted as "the most extensive collection of secondary research resources in the business.") Of the professionals, 96 are in marketing/advertising research, and 10 are in media research.

This translates into 8.3 professionals per $10 million in gross income, far above the industry average of 5.4. In terms of the percentage of its gross income expended on research operations, BBDO is believed to have one of the largest percentages of all large U.S. agencies, if not the largest.

At BBDO there is the traditional research group, headed by either a research director or an associate director, assigned to each account. The senior research person also is a member of a Brand Planning Group which includes the responsible individual from creative, account management, media, and senior management; this group, which overlaps the traditional agency account structure, has major coordinating responsibility for a given brand.

In addition, at BBDO NY, there is a Marketing Sciences Group of 25 people headed by R. Dale Wilson, which is responsible for marketing model development, computer operations, and new product forecasting and analysis.

A third group, Marketing Horizons, is responsible for monitoring changing life-style trends and "futures research." A fourth group, Special Projects, is charged with the development and improvement of techniques used by BBDO research, broad-scale consumer attitude and life-style research, and BBDO position papers on research questions.

In-house facilities include "Hotline," a 10-station WATS phone facility in the New York office, as well as "Ad-Lab," a focus group facility.

Regarding hiring research staff, an agency statement says, "We value integrity and the kind of personal strength that makes integrity possible. We value hard-working people, people who love advertising and the challenge it offers. We value intellect and creativity, and find it difficult to distinquish between the two." BBDO does some recruiting direct from graduate schools ("That's where you find the brains"), and transfer from research into other agency functions is discouraged.

Lewis G. Pringle, 41, is executive vice president/director of research services, at BBDO. He joined the agency in 1968 and was elected to the Board of Directors in 1978. Mr. Pringle is a graduate of Harvard University and received his Ph D from the Massachusetts Institute of Technology.

LEO BURNETT USA — Chicago

Burnett, the largest agency in Chicago and the 6th largest in the U.S. with a gross income of $124 million in 1981, can lay claim to the largest agency research staff under one roof — 136, of whom 100 are professionals. (This figure does not include three librarians or about 54 part-timers associated with the department.)

That works out to 8.1 professionals per $10 million gross income, the third highest among major agencies.

The Burnett operation is distinctive in other respects. For one, since mid-year 1981, researchers assigned to creative actually have offices in the creative department to promote close, day-to-day cooperation and rapport. Also, Burnett pioneered 25 years ago the use of central location interviewing. (Today, the Burnett facility is located near a mall in a Chicago suburb. A focus-group facility is located in the agency's main office in Chicago's Loop.)

According to an agency spokesman, "Virtually all of our research is conducted in-house, except for field work done outside Chicago." A Burnett Lifestyle Program, started in 1967, monitors societal changes and their relevance to advertising problems.

"While we deal with a great range and variety of research," says a spokesman, "five areas account for the majority of our projects: focus-group discussions, copy research, life-styles analysis, the planning/evaluation of new product introductory programs, and experimental work to improve our understanding of how advertising works — and to find better tools for studying the ways people are affected by advertising."

Organizationally, Burnett assigns each account a research group headed by a vice president/group research director (who is physically located in the creative department), who is backed up by associates and analysts. In addition, there are four groups of specialists: (1) Qualitative Research (focus groups, depth interviews); (2) New Product Research (tracking studies, study of new-product introductory copy); (3) Consumer and Marketing Research Programs (life-style program and the modeling of relationships between advertising and sales/purchase behavior); and (4) Copy Development Research (R&D on copy testing procedures).

Burnett research recruits staff from universities. Also, the agency's client service department, as part of its training program, puts recruits into research for a year or so.

Head of Burnett research is Calvin W. Gage, 51, senior vice president/director of research, who joined the agency in 1955. He has a Master's degree in American studies from the University of Minnesota.

FOOTE, CONE & BELDING COMMUNICATIONS — Chicago

FCB has six research units: FCB-Chicago; FCB-New York; FCB-Honig, San Francisco; FCB/Honig-Los Angeles; Aitkin-Kynett-Philadelphia; and Deutsch, Shea & Evans. In toto, these autonomous units employ 112 people in research, of whom 79 are professionals. Since the total FCB gross income in the United States in 1981 was $116.5 million, this works out to 6.8 professionals per $10 million in income, well above the industry average. (These numbers do not include an additional 18 staffers who work in FCB's information center in Chicago, a depository of secondary research materials.)

FCB research is distinctive in terms of the emphasis put on operating philosophy, the gist of which is embodied in a 17-page policy statement entitled "The Role of Research at FCB." The operative statement is, "FCB researchers work on advertising strategies and advertising. Advertising is their subject, not research. Research is the tool of the trade." Also, there is an emphasis on timing: "Research early in the creative process — delivered fast before decisions have had to be made without the research — can become part of the solution of even the most difficult advertising problems. But late research delivered slowly, can instead compound advertising problems."

FCB claims a battery of 30 different research techniques "which have been invented, developed, extended or adapted to become FCB tools of research." These are viewed as the "minimum capability" of each research group. An illustration of such "tools" is Diagnostic Copy Test, an evaluative procedure (mostly face-to-face interviews in a mall setting) for rough and developmental copy. Along this line, FCB research made news by underwriting an on-air TV commercial testing procedure that they felt was most suitable for evaluating the impact of highly emotional copy treatments, with emphasis on non-verbal communications, rather than the traditional day-after-recall techniques that tend to place most emphasis on a respondent's ability to feed back (i.e., verbalize) key copy points or a selling proposition.

Results of this study were presented to the whole advertising agency community via a series of meetings in major cities.

Organizationally, FCB research staff is divided into teams, headed by either an associate research director or research supervisor, which then have account assignments. A media research group is headed by Hugh Zielske.

In addition, FCB maintains in its Chicago office a focus-group facility which has its own staff.

Head of FCB research is David Berger, 54, senior vice president, corporate director of research, who has been with the agency since 1959, part of the time in account management work. A graduate of Columbia University, Mr. Berger also has an MBA degree from Harvard Business School. He is a member of the FCB Strategy Board.

J. WALTER THOMPSON USA — New York

JWT-USA had a gross income from U.S. operations of $153.7 million in 1981, ranking it third in size. (This is not to be confused with the parent company, J. Walter Thompson Group, which includes among other properties Hill & Knowlton, the world's largest public relations agency, which has a sizable research department of its own, and Simmons Market Research Bureau, the staffs of which are not included in this analysis).

JWT-USA employs 106 people in research in six offices; 83 of these are professionals, so that works out to 5.4 professionals per $10 million in gross income, average for large agencies.

"The research operation at JWT, as the name Research and Planning signifies, goes well beyond data collection," I've been told. "It is functionally integrated into the agency's Target Planning System. Department professionals work with the account team on a continuing basis in the planning, development, execution, and evaluation stages of marketing and communications strategies for our clients," says a spokesperson. Researchers are organized on an account group basis, with client assignments, and the lead researcher is a member of the agency's Target Planning Team.

JWT says its commitment to research is "most strongly demonstrated through its long-standing investment in a continuing R&D program." As examples of this, JWT cites the following: a study of the public's perception of television violence and its effects upon the performance of advertising; a "new demographics" for defining the changing role of women — and responses to traditional and contemporary portrayals of women in advertising; tracking studies of consumer responsiveness to generic products; and a study of the potential value of long-form commercials available upon demand via "Cableshop."

In addition to account group assignees, JWT research staffers are organized into groups of functional expertise: media research, statistical analysis, sampling, marketing models, forecasting, information retrieval, etc. Some consultants are used on an as-needed basis.

JWT has semi-annual, two-day seminars, which are attended by the senior research professionals from its U.S. offices as well as its affiliated U.S. and Canadian operations. The purpose: share research expertise and ideas.

Sonia Yuspeh, who joined JWT in 1972, is senior vice president in charge of research and planning. In 1982 she was appointed chairwoman of the agency's U.S. Research & Development Committee. She also chairs the New York office Strategy Plans Board. Ms. Yuspeh took a Master's degree in sociology from Cornell University.

TED BATES & CO. — New York

Bates was the fourth largest U.S. agency in 1981 with a gross income of $129.1 million (excluding Wm. Esty, a recent acquisition). In addition to the parent company, Bates today includes seven subsidiaries, most notably Campbell-Mithun and, recently, Wm. Esty. In toto, these eight organizations employ 99 people in research, 79 of whom are professionals. (About one-half of this staff is with Bates/NY.) For all Bates properties, this works out to 4 professionals per $10 million in income. However, the calculation for Bates/NY alone is 6.5, and for all the other properties combined, 2.9. (These counts do not include nine librarians employed by these agencies.)

As for Bates/NY, the research staff is two and one-half times as large today as it was in 1980 when John A. Fiedler came from Leo Burnett to be senior vice president/executive research director. Further, the professional staff today, with a couple of exceptions, is new to Bates since 1980.

As for philosophy, the new stance goes like this: "The mission of Bates Research is implicit in the agency's philosophy and discipline, the U.S.P. Explicitly, our goal is to help get better copy, quicker."

Structurally, Bates research in New York is divided into four operating units: (1) four Professional Groups, each headed by a vice president/research director, which have client assignments; (2) the Marketing Sciences and Services Group, overseeing research development activities and liaison with the academic research community; (3) Research Operations Group, which is responsible for the fielding of research studies, coding and tabulating; and (4) the Information Services Group, which has direct computer access to over 50 major data bases.

In addition to the line organization, the Bates department is simultaneously organized into five specialized task forces ("probably a misapplication of matrix management," according to Mr. Fiedler), to wit: Motivation Research Group headed by Rudy Schroeer and Jack Bookbinder; the Test Marketing Experimental Design Group headed by Paul Keller; the Copy Research Group headed by Sheri Nadel; and the Market Structure and Segmentation Research Group headed by David Gantman.

The Bates department periodically issues a report, New Product Scan, which monitors all new products in test market and national launch. It has worked closely with Stanford Research in the design and execution of their Values and Lifestyles Research Program. In addition, Bates has worked with the Music and Marketing Departments of Columbia University on studies regarding the effect of music in advertising. Also, in conjunction with SUNY-Purchase, the agency has begun experimental research in the area of psychophysics (brainwave activities).

Mr. Fielder, 40, received his MBA degree from the University of Chicago and is a member of the Bates Board.

DOYLE DANE BERNBACH, INC. — New York

DDB, which includes eight different operating groups in the United States, had a gross income of $115 million from U.S. operations in 1981, ranking it eighth among agencies in size. There are 82 people (mostly headquartered in New York) working in research — 71 in advertising and marketing research, 11 in media research. Of these, 62 are professionals, and that works out to 5.4 per $10 million in income, right near the industry average. (This does not include eight staffers in the agency's research library, which features on-line terminal access to various data banks.)

This staff is organized into two groups, with one reporting to a vice president/manager of research (Sy Collins), and another reporting to a vice president/manager of marketing services. Under research, there are six group research directors, each a vice president, and each of these has a staff of professionals with titles such as associate group director, research supervisor, etc. Each group has a list of client assignments, except for one that specializes in international research and special agency projects. (Some members of the marketing services staff are involved in secondary research, and these are included in the counts above.)

In addition to conducting a wide range of day-to-day studies — from brand image to media mix and weight studies, from legal support to product test, and a variety of copy development tests in conjunction with DDB's creative staff — the DDB research group has developed several techniques that they feel to be innovative. For instance: METER, a TV pre-testing technique called Multiple Exposure Television Effectiveness Research; CON-TEST, a system to test alternative advertising strategies; GOALS, a five-step systematic, disciplined approach to the Generation of Advertising Leverage Strategies; and two unique systems for measuring the "intrusiveness" of radio commercials and the readership of print ads (which includes a mock newspaper where test ads can be tipped in).

The top research executive at DDB is Ruth Ziff, executive vice president and director/research & marketing services. Prior to joining DDB in 1979, she was vice president and manager of research at Benton & Bowles. Ms. Ziff is a member of the agency's Management Review Board and a director of DDB. She received a PhD in sociology from The City College of New York and, in 1973, was named Advertising Woman of the Year by the American Advertising Federation.

GREY ADVERTISING, INC. — New York

Grey, with an estimated $94.4 million in U.S. gross income, ranked ninth among agencies in 1981. The agency has 76 people working in marketing, advertising, and media research (of whom 47 are professionals) in four offices: New York, Chicago, Los Angeles, and San Francisco. This works out to 5 research professionals per $10 million in income, slightly below the industry average.

Beyond that, the Grey research setup is distinctively different from that of other major agencies. For one, Grey solicits studies from organizations that are not Grey clients for advertising. Also, Grey research has a long-standing, contractual relationship with Data Development Corporation, (New York) to handle the fielding of all Grey studies, including the pre-testing of TV commericals through the "Pre-Search" methodology utilized by Grey. Data processing is done on Grey's in-house computer, and, of course, analysis and presentation are handled by Grey's professional staff. Consequently, Grey positions itself as a "full-service" research organization that conducts large-scale surveys for clients in addition to the normal consultation to clients and internal agency staff.

Organizationally, Grey research has a group of nine associate research directors, each of whom — along with backup analytical staff — has responsibility for all primary research done for his/her account assignments, regardless of the type of study involved. In addition, under a separate manager, Grey offers a continuous Consumer Social Trend Analysis service. This group monitors behavioral trends, from secondary sources, and prepares reports for client and internal consumption.

There are three internal department functions that provide backup to this staff: (1) research operations — data collection supervision and control, in-house EDP; (2) technical operations — under the supervision of an outside consultant, Leland E. Ott — provides sampling and multivariate statistical services; and (3) an information center maintains a file of secondary research data on all aspects of the agency and client businesses (the staff of which is not included in the counts above).

In the United States, Grey Research executes about $5 million in custom primary consumer research volume a year, including projects done outside the United States but processed through New York.

Head of the Grey research operation is Barbara S. Feigin, senior vice president/director of marketing and research, who has been with the agency since 1969. Previously, she held research management posts at Marplan and Benton & Bowles. Born in Berlin, Germany, Ms. Feigin has a BA degree from Whitman College (where she is on the Board of Overseers) and has completed a graduate program in business administration at the Harvard Business School.

NEEDHAM, HARPER & STEERS ADVERTISING, INC. — Chicago / New York

Although it ranked 20th among U.S. agencies in 1981 in U.S. gross income ($59.2 million), NH&S ranks eighth in terms of the size of its research staff (74, of whom 53 are professionals) and first in terms of the number of research professionals per $10 million in income — 9 as compared to a large agency average of 5.4.

There are five NH&S offices in the United States, but most of the research staff is located in the largest — Chicago and New York. These operations, apparently, are completely autonomous with Chicago headed by William D. Wells, senior vice president/director of marketing services, and New York headed by Jacqueline Silver, senior vice president/director of research. They are described as "peers," and each has the responsibility for guiding the strategic planning activities in his/her respective office.

"NH&S is often thought of for its campaigns that have the ability to touch human emotion through both 'the heart and the head.' We believe our advertising reaches out because our knowledge of the target is both complete and insightful," says an agency spokesperson.

Structurally, NH&S stresses multivariate statistical and forecasting procedures. "This area is so important at NH&S," the agency says, "that we have implemented a special group [headed by James C. Crimmins], which is concentrating on model development."

In addition to day-to-day consultation with clients and the design and execution of research studies, NH&S also stresses its annual Life Style Study, which focuses on changing attitudes, trends, and product usage patterns. This study is now in its seventh year.

Mr. Wells, who joined NH&S in Chicago in 1974, received his PhD from Stanford University. Ms. Silver joined NH&S in New York in 1976.

D'ARCY-MacMANUS & MASIUS

DM&M has research departments in each of its seven U.S. offices, and, in total, they employ 70 people, 47 of whom are professionals. Since DM&M gross income for the United States in 1981 was $73.9 million, this works out to 6.4 professionals per $10 million in income, well above the industry average of 5.4 for large agencies. (DM&M owns a research company, Mid-America Research, Mount Prospect, Illinois, which specializes in central location interviewing through four mall sites. Mid-America staff is not included in this analysis.)

Each of the DM&M research staffs operates autonomously, and there is no one person within the DM&M organization who is, at least, the titular head of research. However, the research directors from these seven locations are members of DM&M's Research Operating Committee, which meets quarterly to exchange ideas and consult on problems of common interest.

DM&M, not surprisingly, finds virtue in the decentralization of research, namely that each office tends to have a different type of client base — packaged goods, durables, industrial, etc. — and hence each office can staff/adjust accordingly.

DM&M operating philosophy stresses "up-front research — used developmentally — on behalf of all clients — as the most effective and efficient deployment of resources," according to an agency spokesperson.

The DM&M units do share a central information services department — including central library (librarians are not included in the staff counts above), and there is information retrieval through CRTs. Also, a "New Products Prediction Model" called RAM, which was developed by DM&M Chicago, is available to all DM&M clients. Two of the DM&M offices have life-style researchers on staff, and there are arrangements with several universities as consultants in special areas such as statistics, psychology, and sociology.

DM&M research directors are: Tom Kutsko, Atlanta; Lucien DiSalvo, Bloomfield Hills, Michigan; Marshall Ottenfeld, Chicago; George Scott, Minneapolis; Patricia Greenwald, New York; and Philip Baker, St. Louis. (The San Francisco post is open.)

Part III

The Future

Chapter 15

Looking Ahead

When you can measure what you are speaking of and express it in numbers, you know what you are discoursing. But when you cannot measure it and express it in numbers, your knowledge is of a very meager and unsatisfactory kind.

Lord William T. Kelvin (1824-1907)
British mathematician and physicist

The material in this book attests to the important, and integral, role of marketing and advertising research in the marketing of goods and services and the economic penalties that come from ignoring feedback from the consumer, as documented by good research. As the chairman of American Motors Corporation, Paul Tippett, put it: "Every time — every single time — we've ignored it, for reasons that seemed convenient at the time, we've lived to regret it."

If anything, I sense, the interdependency of marketing and research has thickened during the economic recession of 1981-82. In the late 1970s especially, the seemingly endless availability of cheap and easy money encouraged marketers to go ahead with marginal new product/service ventures. The down-side penalties for failure — or missing predicted success — were not necessarily deadly. But with the recession and extraordinarily high interest rates, the penalty for failure could, indeed, be deadly. To deny the consumer a place at the new product planning conference — by ignoring marketing research — had become just too dangerous. The need to reduce the risk of failure had, in many companies, become paramount.

Partly because of this shift in attitude, partly to become more competitive, partly to induce a cutting edge, avant-garde, "state-of-the-art" image, and partly to reduce costs, many aggressive marketing research service firms offered up to management an avalanche of new services and techniques during the late 1970s and early 1980s. The names of these new services, if nothing else, demonstrated the industry's creativity in developing acronyms. But beyond that, the main thrust of many of these new methodologies/services was predictability — new, sharper, or just more esoteric methods of making early, up-front estimates of a new product's ultimate sales potential. Also enjoying a boom were marketing models used to simulate a potential marketing environment, and permitting quick, relatively inexpensive experimentations in mixes of variables, and closed system marketing laboratories, which come close to providing 360-degree measures of the marketing and advertising environment in which a product can be tested.

These and kindred developments have enjoyed a boomlet as marketing research emphasis seems to move away from past-tense measures to estimates, however crude, of things to come. Despite progress, we should heed the words of Niels Bohr (1885-1962), the famous Danish atomic physicist: "Prediction is very difficult, especially about the future."

A trend running parallel to all this is the embrace, by marketing research practitioners, of new (to marketing research) technology that offers to make data collection quicker, more accurate in some respects, and certainly more independent of man/woman labor. Recent breakthroughs in technology in other fields often are adaptable to data collection problems, and, at least theoretically, they promise some enormous breakthroughs in the understanding of consumer response to marketing and advertising inducements. They also promise an absolute deluge of fresh, timely data that — for all practical purposes — could overwhelm the ability of analysts to sift and sort for specific answers to specific problems.

Beyond that, there's the old saw — "The supply of truth far exceeds the demand." To some extent, that is still the situation in marketing although, as noted earlier, the high cost of failure, especially in the recent recession, has brought many more converts — at least temporarily — to the front of the research preacher's tent asking for a laying on of the hands. But total, absolute, wholehearted convergence of marketing into research, and research into marketing, I suggest, will not come to be until two things happen. The first, and most important by my reckoning, is urging would-be practitioners of marketing (and advertising) research to start their apprenticeship with hands-on experience in the gritties of marketing — field sales, merchandising, packaging, and the workaday chores associated with media buying and the creation of advertising within an agency. Far, far too many research practitioners today are one dimensional and, all too often, fail to fully relate their efforts to those of the total marketing scheme, or their personal insights to those of the total marketing team.

The other thing is that would-be marketing people be forced to do an apprenticeship in a research department or agency. There is nothing more sobering or enlightening than having to actually grip a conceptual sampling problem, experience the chuckholes of data collection in the field, or try to divine out of mountains of statistical tabs those few powerful pieces of information that make or break a marketing decision. It's all easier said than done, and most consumers of marketing research input are blithefully ignorant of the process, or discipline, behind good research studies.

Idealistic? Not at all. Astonishing? Yes, especially if you subscribe to this observation attributed to Ralph Waldo Emerson (1803-1882), the famous American essayist: "Nothing astonishes man as much as common sense."

Indeed, given the amount of money that is paid for marketing and advertising research, and the latent potential it has to enhance the marketing fortunes of an organization, it seems eminently sensible to properly train those involved in its preparation and consumption. Why develop ever more powerful, sophisticated, and complex fighter planes — and then skimp or ignore entirely the training of pilots who can optimize their use? Yet, that's pretty much the situation today in marketing research. Some companies, I'm sure, have started to perceive this and, in their own way, have started to address the problem. Others will follow.

When I was forced to settle on a simple title for this book, the answer, obviously, was *Marketing/Research People: Their Behind-the-Scenes Stories.* That pragmatic goal, I trust, was realized. In doing so, I wanted the events — and the key people involved — to tell the story. Collectively, their stories realistically describe the state of the marketing art today as it is practiced in the United States, and — I trust obviously — there is still an ample element of by guess and by golly. That is the point of departure because, as in other sectors of human endeavor, there is bound to be progress, refinement of technique, and — every now and then — really significant breakthroughs. But, no matter how much more sophisticated marketing and marketing research come to be in the future, I'm inclined to agree with this sentiment written by William Maynard, executive vice president and managing director of creative services at Ted Bates Worldwide, the large New York based advertising agency: "Major clients can't survive without research. There's a need to probe, measure, sort, count; to get the facts and turn them into strategy. But you can't print the research. You have to leave room for the magic to happen. Then bring back research to find out if the magic works."

In the final analysis, it is people who make magic — in advertising, marketing, or research.